MYRON MIXON'S
BBQ RULES

MYRON MIXON'S
BBQ RULES

the OLD-SCHOOL GUIDE *to* SMOKING MEAT

with KELLY ALEXANDER

STEWART, TABORI AND CHANG, NEW YORK

This book is dedicated to
MY DAD, JACK MIXON,

AND TO THE OTHER EARLY PITMASTERS
who helped pave the way for me.

TABLE *of* CONTENTS

CHAPTER 2: THE HOG

CHAPTER 3: BIRDS

CHAPTER 4: THE COW

CHAPTER 5: EXTRAS

The early American pitmasters were

SURVIVORS

trying to make their way in this new country.
And with pit barbecue they hit a home run right off the bat. The best
combination of flavors today is still vinegar, salt, and pepper.

THE RULES FOR BBQ RULES

This is a book that will talk about fire and meat. It will give you trustworthy formulas for many simple preparations of foods like pork, chicken, and beef. But there are a few things you need to keep in mind before you get started. One: I believe smoking meat on a coal-fired masonry pit makes the best barbecue there is.

Before we even get to the first point, you should understand that this book is not about cooking with a direct flame, otherwise known as cooking meat over an open flame, otherwise known as grilling. In this book I'm talking about **barbecuing**. Both methods involve cooking outside. But the similarities to what I'm doing and grilling end there. Grilling is cooking food fast over high heat: 350 to 400°F (175 to 205°C) and up. It's a technique made for meat that's relatively tender and quick to cook. There are lots of good books that can tell you how to do that, but not this one. I specialize in true barbecuing, otherwise known as **smoking** and **pit smoking** (both of which involve cooking meat over fire but rely on different types of heat, which I'll get to in a moment), which not only cooks the meat at 350°F (175°C) or lower, but also infuses and tenderizes the meat with smoke and other natural flavors that can only come from cooking food by means of either direct or indirect wood-fired heat. You should know that, unlike a traditional smoker, a pit offers direct heat: The heat source is placed directly beneath the meat with no barrier—except for the occasional grate—between the coals and the meat. (Traditional smoking, however, is cooking food slowly over a low temperature that is fueled by the heat emitting from smoking wood chips in a vessel we call a *smoker;* there is technically no fire in the smoking process because you're burning embers. When you cook in a masonry pit, there's a fire to stoke.) This book is going to show you how to do that at a level that will make your neighbors weep with admiration and envy, like mine do.

RULE 1:

TRY MAKING YOUR OWN COALS

We are cooking everything in a masonry pit that is fired by coals we'll make our-selves out of fresh wood we source locally. That may sound intimidating, but it's a very easy and inexpensive process that I'm going to talk you through in its entirety. (I will also give alternative recipes for other smokers for many of the dishes.) Turn to *page 38* to see my precise pit setup instructions. (Or turn to *page 44* for tips and advice on modern smokers.)

RULE 2:

WHEN THE PIT IS HOT, COOK A BUNCH OF THINGS

Once you commit to a session of coal-fired pit cooking, you should cook as many things as possible so you make the most out of your time and the heat in the pit. It takes about three hours to get a pit up and running to where you've burned your wood into coals and you've used those coals to heat the pit: Now it's ready for cooking. I say once you've spent three hours getting your pit going, why not take advantage by cooking a bunch of stuff in it? Are you making a brisket? Might as well smoke some cheese in there too, throw in a pork shoulder, or toss a belly on the coals so you can make barbecue sandwiches. The inside of a pit is larger than the inside of a commercial oven and probably larger than the inside of your backyard smoker or grill, even if you're working with professional equipment.

ONE: You have room to cook multiple things at the same time, so do it if you can. TWO: You can scale the amounts in the recipes I'm giving you to suit your needs. Don't need a 20-pound (9-kg), 5-bone prime rib this time? Get a 10-pound (4.5-kg), 3-bone one instead, and adjust the cooking time. (Don't change the technique, just alter the cooking time. My rule of thumb is that you need to cook the meat to the same internal temperature I describe in the larger-sized recipes, just reduce the cooking time by 30 minutes per pound of meat.)

RULE 3:

KEEP THE HEAT CONSISTENT

Don't open your pit or your smoker if you don't have to. Every time you open it, you lower the temperature inside by about 5°F (3°C) for every minute it's open. It'll take several additional minutes of cooking time to make up for that loss of heat. When you're cooking barbecue it's very important to maintain a consistent temperature inside the pit.

RULE 4:

LET THE MEAT REST

When you take it out of the pit, let the meat rest, loosely covered in a pan or on a cutting board. It has to rest after you cook it so that the flavors you worked so hard to infuse concentrate, the texture solidifies, and the temperature regulates throughout the piece of meat. Never skip this step, no matter how much of a hurry you may be in to eat.

THE TRUE STORY OF BARBECUE

I am going to tell you the story of how I got into barbecue, which includes the story of the art form that we today call barbecue plus the story of how I learned to barbecue from my daddy, Jack Mixon. That's a lot of story, and it's going to involve an idea that I think gets overused a lot, one I don't often refer to and sure don't take lightly, and that is "old school." Some people in the world of barbecue claim the term "old school" just because they're cooking with wood ("stick burning," as we call it), but that's not the real deal. In barbecue, old school means cooking on a homemade coal-fried masonry pit, where the first step is burning down wood to make your own coals, then shoveling those coals beneath the meat, and finally cooking that meat over direct heat. That's old school. And that's the way I learned how to do it and how I'll teach you how to do right here, right now.

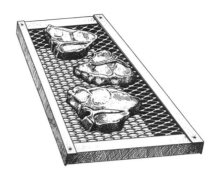

The first experience I had cooking something like what you'd call "barbecue" was with my dad when I was a kid, and it wasn't at the pits where he barbecued for his take-out business. It was when he allowed me to cook a steak at home on our grill. Every Saturday night, we always had steak. And the steak of choice for Jack Mixon was a T-bone. I was probably eight or nine years old when he allowed me to cook the steaks for supper one night on our charcoal grill. Well, that was a big responsibility for me because my dad, Jack, he was pretty damn tough. He'd tear your ass up for spilling tea at the table. All I could think about was what he would do if I messed up his steaks.

But I was also intrigued enough to want to do it anyway, mostly because it was something I never got to do before in my life—and, you know, at eight or nine years old, I hadn't been here long enough to do all that much, so this was exciting. And I wanted to show my dad that I could do it. But little did I know then that there was no way, short of turning the steaks into charcoal, that I could mess them up because Daddy liked his steaks well done—cooked until they were dead. Needless to say, they turned out great. And from that point forward, I was interested in anything to do with fire, and especially when that fire was cooking meat.

At the pit as a young'un with my dad, Jack Mixon.

About Hog Cooking

I have been called "The Best Hog Cooker in the World," and, no lie, I think it's true. I have a unique history with the animal, having grown up around folks who were barbecuing it since before I can remember. And in barbecue competitions, pork has always been a winning category for me. This is in part because the natural sweetness in the meat pairs so nicely with the fruit woods I like to use in my fire. When I got started cooking barbecue, the top dog on the competition circuit was Pat Burke and his Tower Rock BBQ team from Murphysboro, Illinois, and I took inspiration from him. He wasn't playing around drinking and partying at contests—he was working hard instead. His team members were not hobbyists, no sir, and they were there to cook and make money.

At the time I started cooking in competitions, I focused on my hogs because I'd seen my dad do them countless times in our own pits. I had to learn, though, how to take my knowledge and turn it into something that could impress those folks judging the contests. At Memphis in May events, whole hog is the key category. You are visited in person at your cooking site by a judge who sits down, chats, and judges your hog on taste, tenderness, and appearance. I decided on a hog-cooking philosophy early on, which is to focus on helping my meat taste like meat, and not like grape jelly or maple syrup or any of the other so-called secret ingredients my competitors claim.

So even though I've learned a whole lot about presentation and making up the beautiful-looking Styrofoam boxes of pork we submit to judges at contests, I've held on to my simple philosophy of taste since the beginning, and it's been a winner: Great pork barbecue should have the flavor of the meat coming through first and foremost, it should be moist and tender, and it should have layers of flavor when you eat it. The first layer is the natural flavor of the meat. The second is the flavors it picks up from the salt, pepper, and vinegar you seasoned it with before you cooked it. The third layer comes from the smoke that enters the meat from the burning of the wood you've selected and turned into coals. Smoke and meat: That's what makes pork become that thing we know and love as "barbecue."

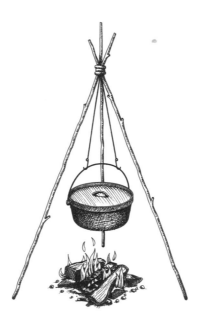

THE FIRST PITMASTERS

I was raised shoveling coals under masonry pits, and I thought that was the only way that barbecue was done—I thought that was the norm. Little did I know that what I was doing as a kid was an ancient form of cooking that came from the time the forefathers of this country first started barbecuing. (My first realization that coal-fired pit barbecue was an unusual throwback type of cooking didn't happen until I was in my teens, when I started noticing that everybody else but our family and a few others in town had the kind of metal cookers like the ones I use now at competitions.)

We know man has been cooking meat over fire since the dawn of time, and we know that the people who first came to this country did the same. They were just trying to make food to feed themselves and their tribes back then, of course, and they sure weren't trying to become well-known pitmasters or some other title that we like to give ourselves in this day and age, like "grill master," "lord of the grill," or whatever. These gentlemen—and women, too—were trying to feed large families and to do it cheaply with what they had. And they took the livestock they had on the farms and the trees they had surrounding them as their fuel, the wood they needed to burn for their fires, and they used things they had on the farm for seasoning, such as what they'd put up in the root cellar.

Back then you had pepper, you had salt, and you'd distill your own vinegars. That's why today we relate vinegar to Carolina barbecue and southern barbecue in general, because it has been a part of cooking meat down here since people first camped out on this land. The combination of meat and smoke with vinegar-based sauces has been around almost as long as this country has been inhabited. And let's not forget that vinegar has an added benefit: In those days it wasn't just a flavoring agent, but it was also used as a preservative and an important antibacterial agent. So it kept your meat tasting good, and it kept it safe to eat, too. Those early Americans were pretty smart, if you ask me.

So we're talking about necessity here, not about somebody saying, "I want to be a great chef." I'd argue that without this type of barbecuing, we wouldn't have great chefs. That's because the evolution of cooking meat over fire led to our first pitmasters, otherwise known as the people who were in charge of the barbecuing, whether it was in encampments, backyards, little shacks along the side of the road, or, eventually, in proper restaurants. These are the folks who got their start cooking on the grounds at the local churches or for the politicians' fund-raisers. These people became very well known and respected in southern communities because they were the keepers of the fire. That was a pitmaster. Back then the title meant respect. These people learned their art; they learned how to select meats, they learned how to select the woods they wanted to use, and they learned how to manage fire. Today, "pitmaster" usually refers to people cooking on TV more than it corresponds to a respected community leader. Let's change that right here and now.

Now, recall that barbecuing isn't just about cooking meat and turning out food. It's about family; it's about the people around you when you eat it and the shared experience of enjoying it. Barbecue is the most social food we have. What I mean by "social food" is that I never heard of anybody eating barbecue all alone; that's probably why "barbecue" means both a style of cooking and also the event where that style of food is eaten. When you say "barbecue" in the South you're likely referring to the type of events that support communities and raise money for a whole range of causes, like local church groups and Little League teams and stumping politicians. Some of us southerners have historically had barbecue at our wedding receptions. Now I see that our trend is spreading around the country, in part I think because barbecue just lends itself to gatherings and togetherness. The flavors of the rural South can be found proudly displayed at occasions all over the country, not just the ones in our own backyards down here. It tickles me that the people who used to want white tablecloths and finger sandwiches cut out like little moons and stars or whatever at their weddings are now calling up pitmasters like me, asking us to bring our own homegrown legacies to their celebrations. That's how social barbecue is: It's the thing to eat at parties everywhere. And what's more, pitmasters today are once again important parts of their communities. Hell, I became mayor of Unadilla, Georgia.

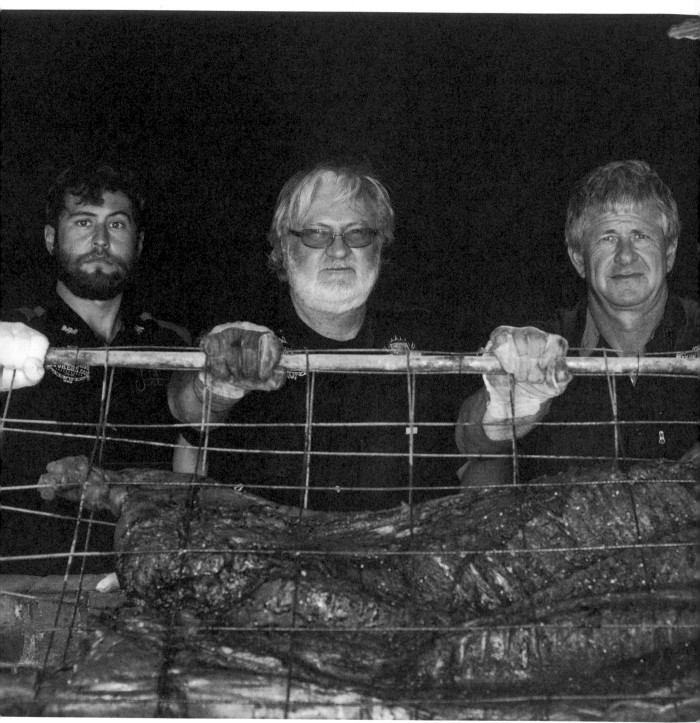

Three generations of pitmasters: my son Michael, me, my brother Tracy, and my mother's brother Charles Cross.

ABOUT THE RECIPES IN THIS BOOK

I am going to take you back to the way real barbecue is done here, like I've promised, and I'm going to do that through my recipes. There are no complicated recipes with exotic ingredients in this book. Because that's not what early barbecue was about, and even today it shouldn't be about anything "complex." Barbecue is a simple food, and it was always intended to be that way. It's about meat, it's about smoke, and it's about fire: That's all it's about. I think that sometimes, some celebrity chefs get out in the world and try to justify their salaries by making barbecue out to be something I don't think it was intended to be. It's supposed to be something you can do, and do very well, in your own backyard.

I tell a lot of people who come to my cooking schools that there's nothing wrong with putting your stamp on your food, with trying to make a little tweak here or there to make the barbecue unique. But I caution you that whatever spice rub or sauce you concoct for yourself, try to keep some form of balance there, something that relates to this old-school way of doing things. I say keep to the lines of tradition. I'm not saying you've always got to make the strict traditional coal-fired masonry pit–style barbecue I was raised on—consisting mostly of salt, pepper, and vinegar for flavoring—but try to keep it simple as much as you can. What I'm saying is that just because you can do something with a piece of meat doesn't necessarily mean you need to do that. For example, I love chocolate cake and I love spareribs—but I don't necessarily want my spareribs to taste like chocolate cake.

That's a little bit of me on a soapbox right there, but to me barbecue's not just about cooking food—it's my life, and it was a big part of my dad's life, and it's been a big part of my family's life for a long time. The thing is, if you ride through south Georgia right now, especially in the more rural areas, I guarantee that in 90 percent of the yards you drive past there will be some sort of smoker or grill or pit—and that's just the way it is, that's the way we were raised down here. You have a car, you have a tractor in the barn, and you have a smoker in your backyard. These are the accessories of living in the South. We take barbecue for granted a lot, and most of us were unaware that everybody else didn't enjoy what we do until recently.

Now, though, barbecue has been put out there in front of the country, as a matter of fact in front of the whole world, and it's a cool thing. Right now if you look around, especially on TV, everything that's popular revolves around the South. I think everybody's intrigued by ideas about the southern lifestyle, and a big part of that southern lifestyle is barbecue. And barbecue itself is a lifestyle. I believe that firmly, because I learned it from my dad, who learned it from his dad, who learned it from his dad, right on down through the generations, stretching from the time the Mixon family first hit the shores of Jamestown, Virginia, in 1650. It's how we live; it's what we do. And now I'm going to teach it to you.

Celebrating a win early on with my son Michael and members of the Jack's Old South team.

How Much Have I Won?

I entered my first barbecue competition, the Lock-&-Dam BBQ Contest in Augusta, Georgia, six months after my father died in January 1996. I did it mostly to see if I could sell some of the bottled sauce my parents were making and selling, get a little name recognition out there for our brand. I took first place in the whole-hog category, first place in the ribs category, and third place in the pork shoulder category. At my first contest ever. Once I got a taste of how successful I could be at competitive barbecue, I never looked back; I entered as many contests as I could, pushing myself to make better and more delicious barbecue all along the way.

Early days on the competition circuit.

Since then, I've won more barbecue competitions than anyone else in the world, and I have earned more than $1 million in prize money. Here's why you ought to pay attention to what I say: Since 1996, I've won more than two hundred grand championships, thirty state championships (including wins in Georgia, Florida, Alabama, Virginia, Arkansas, Mississippi, Kentucky, Illinois, South Carolina, and Tennessee), and eleven national championships, and I've earned more than eighteen hundred trophies. My team has taken three first-place whole-hog awards at the Jack Daniel's World Championship Invitational Barbecue competition, and we have been crowned grand champion at the World Championship in Memphis three times (in 2001, 2004, and 2007). We have also taken first place in the whole-hog category at the World Championship four times (in 2001, 2003, 2004, and 2007). Jack's Old South has been the Memphis in May Team of the Year with the highest number of points for eight years (from 1999 through 2004, and also in 2007 and 2009). We are also the only team to win grand championships in the Memphis in May, Kansas City BBQ Society, and Florida BBQ Association contests in the same year. I was inducted into the Barbecue Hall of Fame in Kansas City in 2013.

CHAPTER 1:

RULES
and
HELPERS

RULES

RULE 1:

USE THE RIGHT WOOD

Now, when I say, "Use the right wood," I'm referring to the process of choosing the type of wood you'll use to smoke your meat, which is the very first step of cooking real pit-smoked barbecue. When I was a kid and it was time to get cooking, our first job was to pick the woods my dad liked, and the woods he liked were, number one, local, meaning whatever grew in south Georgia, and, number two, fresh and green. Jack liked to use a blend of hickory and oak for this style of cooking, and it had to be green, by which I mean young and flexible. Green wood is important because its moisture ensures that when you burn it down for coals, the coals are big and pop off easily. Think of it this way: With today's type of barbecue technology, we all use seasoned wood, because when it cooks down it makes ash (and we find the smoky flavor from that ash desirable); but when we cook old school, we want the wood to burn down and make coals that will have to burn again, and for that process to work well you need to start with green wood.

More about that wood: The best advice I can give you is the advice my dad followed, which is to use what grows close around you. I get asked a lot about the best woods to use for barbecue, and I have my own distinct opinion on that based on my own experience: You already know I'm down in south Georgia, and that my dad taught me how to use a combination of young hickory and oak from the time I was a little boy. Then I got into competitive barbecue, and because I am in the Peach State, I have access to peach wood (I'll sell you some and ship it to you if want—www.jacksoldsouth.com). So I'm also a big fan of peach wood because as I've progressed as a pitmaster I've learned how to blend woods. I like peach wood blended in with what started me out, hickory and oak. When I'm asked about which wood to use, I ask people where they live and what they have around them. If you have access to young green fruit woods, take advantage of them: Apple wood, pear wood, apricot wood, grapevine wood, or cherry wood—any and all of these are great choices for barbecue and should be available locally in your groceries and wherever you can buy a smoker. That's what the first pitmasters did: If they lived in Missouri, they didn't have the option of having peach wood shipped to them like you and I do today. They had to cook with the wood that was around them. So my answer to which wood to use is this: There are a lot of different woods that are great for barbecuing, and what you should use just depends on where you're located and what kind of wood or trees you have in your area.

The very first step of cooking real pit-smoked barbecue is choosing

THE RIGHT WOOD.

And by that I mean local. Use wood that grows around where you live.

RULE 2:

BUILD YOURSELF A PIT

materials and tools

Large heavy-duty shovel

Rake or hoe

Hand tamp

Pick

Tape measure

48 cinder blocks (standard 8 x 8 x 16-inch / 20.5 x 20.5 x 40.5-cm size)

Level

Four 2 x 4-inch (5 x 10-cm) stakes

Masonry sand

Carpenter's square

1 sheet of 48 x 80-inch (122 x 203-cm) expanded metal

2 sheets of 4 x 4-foot (1.2 x 1.2-m) 16-gauge steel

1 sheet of 2 x 4-foot (0.6 x 1.2-m) 16-gauge steel

Building a backyard barbecue pit is about half a day's worth of good hard labor, but it's as straightforward as it gets and doesn't require a high degree of skill. All the materials are available at a good local hardware store or home improvement center, and you can get it all for less than $400.

PICK A SITE

You need a good spot for your pit and its 48 x 80-inch (122 x 203-cm) foundation. You need level ground that is a safe distance (about 20 feet / 6 m) from your house and from any wooden structures like decks or gazebos, and as clear of dry vegetation as possible.

LAY THE GROUNDWORK

Once you've settled on a spot, take your time to use the shovel, rake, and tamp as necessary to level the ground thoroughly. You will need to remove grass, weeds, and rocks from the site. Dig out any high spots in the area; picks and shovels work fine for this.

1) Take 14 cinder blocks and assemble them into a rectangle that is 48 x 80 inches (122 x 203 cm); it will be five cinder blocks long and two cinder blocks wide, as shown.

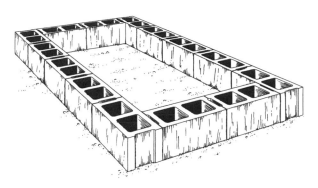

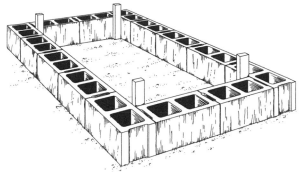

2) Place the 2 x 4-inch (5 x 10-cm) stakes at the four inside corners. Then remove the cinder blocks.

Excavate topsoil from the interior area of the pit (the area inside the stakes) and refill it with the masonry sand—you'll end up removing 4 to 6 inches (10 to 15 cm) of topsoil and replacing it with 4 to 6 inches (10 to 15 cm) of masonry sand.

* Note: That's the basic method, and it will have the grease from what's cooking in the pit run down laterally into the topsoil, which is fine. If you want to do something a little more elegant, you can dig down a full foot (30.5 cm) and grade the excavated area so that any cooking grease will run down to a central point that is 12 inches (30.5 cm) deep—then just refill the hole with sand or line it with fire brick. Again, this is not necessary, but it is a nice feature.

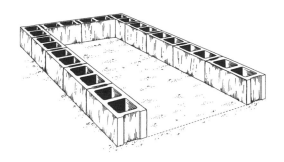

3) Reassemble the first 5 x 2 rectangle of cinder blocks. Decide which of the shorter, two-block ends you want to be the front of the pit and remove those two blocks. This gap will be used to load fresh coals in during the cook, so make sure it's facing an area that provides enough space for you to do something like maneuver a hog gurney and swing a shovel.

LAY THE PIT

4) Stack a second layer of blocks atop the first. Make sure all the blocks line up with those under them and use the carpenter's square to ensure that the two blocks at each corner are flush, then lay the sheet of expanded metal on top of that.

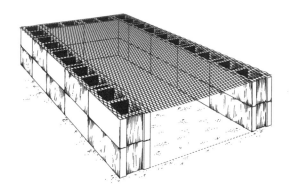

5) Stack two more layers of cinder blocks on top of the expanded metal grill and place the two 4 x 4-foot (1.2 x 1.2-m) steel sheets over the top as a roof. There is going to be a bit of overlap between the sheets as well as over the edges of the pit—that's good. The overlap will allow you to grip the sheet and slide it off when checking on a cook and maintaining the cooking temp in the pit.

6) Finally, set the 2 x 4-foot (0.6 x 1.2-m) steel sheet against the open end of the pit, allowing for ventilation, and that's it. Now you just need some wood (see Use the Right Wood, page 33), meat or different kinds of food to cook on the pit's 10 square feet (0.9 sq m) of grill space, and all your friends.

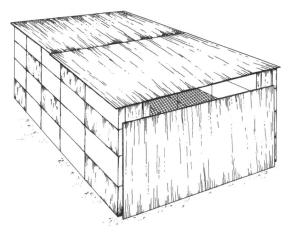

<h1 style="text-align:center">R U L E 3 :</h1>

LEARN TO FIRE THE PIT

Making your own coals is very easy when you understand how the process works. All you need is a 55-gallon (208-L) barrel, green wood, and fire. I make coals by burning the green wood, which contains a significant amount of moisture, in a large heavy barrel until that wood pops off chunks of smoldering wood. Those chunks are going to be your coals. So first you load your barrel with green wood, then you let it burn, and finally the coals fall to the bottom of the barrel, where you have made a hole large enough that you can reach in with a shovel to remove them. Once you have burned your wood and created your own coals, all you need to do is transfer those coals into your pit. Use a long-handled heavy-duty shovel for that job, wear heavy work gloves, and take care not to burn yourself on your way from the barrel to the pit.

LIGHTERED KNOTS

My daddy loved doing everything the old-fashioned way, including lighting fires. This means he lit them using a technique known as "lightered knots." If you want to feel especially authentic, like you may have been the one who invented fire, give it a try: 1) You need dead wood for this, which has the richest resin and is driest to burn. Walk around a forest (or your backyard) and look for old pine trees, which are an excellent source. Once you've found one, saw off a dead branch. This is some high-quality firewood. 2) Using a small sharp knife, carve the branch down to expose the "fatwood," which looks like small, unblemished dry matchsticks. 3) Whittle those shavings of fatwood until they resemble fine chips. 4) Light your chips and aerate properly in order to create a healthy flame. That's old-school fire.

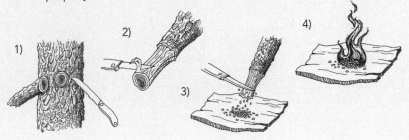

RULE 4:

MAINTAIN CONSISTENT HEAT IN THE PIT

The single most important job for any pitmaster is to manage the fire in the pit and keep the pit temperature consistent. My dad did this with two pieces of old tin he used to cover the pits that could slide back and forth. They were loose enough to allow some smoke to seep out and some oxygen to get in and allow the embers to glow, but tight enough to keep heat inside the chamber. We maintained the temperature by running our hands over the bare tin: If we could hold our hands on that tin for a count of 10 without snatching our hand back, we knew it was time to re-fire the pit. As you can see, we didn't use a thermometer or other kind of gauge to measure the temperature.

In my adulthood I've experimented with the 10-count method: I used a temperature gauge in my pit just to find out what cooking temp my dad was likely maintaining. And that gauge was telling me something around 250 to 275°F (120 to 135°C). So you can use the Jack Mixon 10-Count System, or you can use a temperature gauge; that part is up to you. What's important is mastering the art of keeping the temperature consistent in that pit. Don't get impatient and over-fire and try to get the cooking done quicker, because then you will have a flame-up and when that grease hits too much flame or too many coals down there, it will burn up anything cooking in the pit. About every 30 minutes, run your hand over that tin and see what's what. (If you would like to use a thermometer, check it every 30 minutes and aim for a steady and consistent 250 to 275°F / 120 to 135°C.) If you can rest your hand on the top for 10 seconds (or more), you know it's time to shovel in some new coals. First collect the coals in a canister or in the body of a kettle grill. Light them and get them good and hot. Then use your shovel to transfer the hot coals—always transfer hot coals that are lit into the smoker. Make sure you shovel them right onto the hot coals burning in there so they can keep your temp consistent where it's already been firing.

Final rule for maintaining your heat: Try hard not to let any heat out of the pit if you don't have to; don't open your pit any more than necessary. Remember: Every time you open the pit, you lower the temperature inside by about 5°F (3°C) for every minute it's open, and it takes several additional minutes of cooking time to make up for that loss of heat. A big part of maintaining a consistent temperature is keeping that pit closed as much as you can.

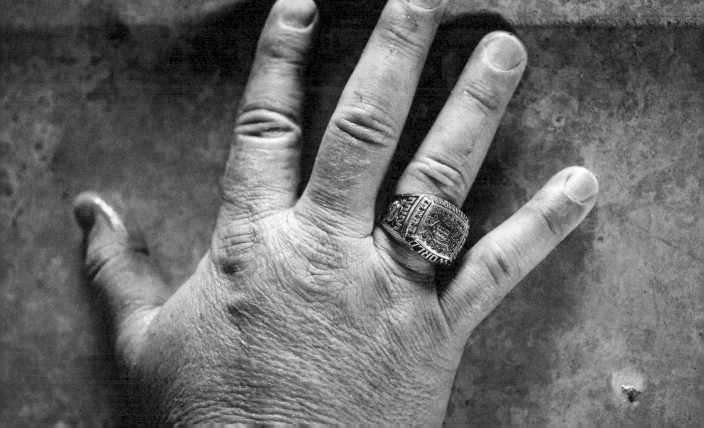

RULE 5:

CHOOSE YOUR FIRE WISELY

The first decision you have to make is what kind of cooker you're going to use. Listen, you don't need competition-level equipment to make excellent barbecue. There is an incredible range of smokers on the market, from the cheap charcoal "bullet" jobs to our top-of-the-line Myron Mixon Smokers (myronmixonsmokers.com), and the best one for you is the one that you feel most comfortable using.

> *Note: I believe there is no substitute for making your own coals and smoking meat in a masonry pit—that's why I'm writing this book, because the particular flavor that process imbues is unique, and once you've tried it you'll be hooked. However, it's not the only way to make good barbecue. Smoking meat in a smoker using a water pan is what I do in competitive barbecue and it results in a more polished product, if you will—it's not as "rough and ready" as pit-smoked barbecue. It is also delicious and prized, but it tastes a little different than the barbecue I grew up eating. And some folks, god bless them, actually prefer it. And as much as I want you to build a pit and learn to cook like my daddy taught me, you can use any one of these options and get a good result if you follow my techniques.

Most American households own a grill, and the most popular type of these is a **gas grill**. If you have a gas grill, you can adapt it to smoke food. Here's what you do: Take your favorite wood chips, put them in a bowl, and cover them with water; let the wood soak overnight. When you're ready to cook, drain the chips, wrap them in one or two packets of foil, and use a fork to poke several holes in the top of each packet; set aside. Close the grill's side vents—don't worry about doing an airtight job of it, just do the best you can to shut them. Now, these days most gas grills have either two or three burners that can be controlled individually. On a two-burner gas grill, light only one side; on a three-burner grill, light the two outside burners and leave the burner in the middle unlit. Place the packet of wood chips on the lit section (or sections); then place the meat on the unlit section and cook it—the flame will smolder the wet wood chips, producing the smoky flavor in your meat.

You can use any recipe in this book designed for a pit in any of these smokers, no problem: They will work perfectly with my recipes. I have always said that there is no need for high-end equipment to make good barbecue. I tell folks who come to my barbecue cooking schools that it's easier to learn on simple equipment and then move on to more advanced types of cookers, so save your money.

HOW A SMOKER WORKS

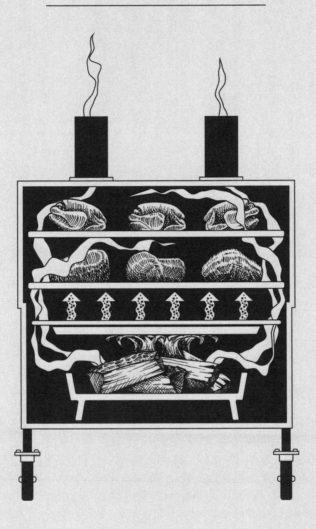

The smoker contains racks that the meat cooks on. The smoker's base is filled with wood to provide heat and smoke. (Sometimes charcoal is used to start the wood burning, or charcoal is used for fuel and wood or wood chips are added on top in a pan—like the one shown above—for smoke.) The smoke flows around the meat on the racks, flavoring it, while the indirect heat cooks it. It's a simple thing.

CHARCOAL GRILL

Charcoal grills are also known as kettle grills. To smoke food instead of grill on this type of equipment, simply soak your wood chips in water overnight, drain them, and set them aside. Start your fire and get your coals nice and hot. Now rearrange your coals so that you bank all of your charcoal on one side of the kettle, leaving a cold area where you'll place your meat. Arrange a grilling rack over your coals. Lay your food on the grill. Finally, place the soaked and drained wood chips directly onto your coals—they'll smoke right up. Place the lid on the kettle, experiment with how much or how little to open the vent on the top of the kettle to regulate the heat, and close the lid and cook.

BULLET SMOKER

A **bullet smoker** is an electric or charcoal smoker and is what most grilling enthusiasts progress to when they first start smoking. It is called a "bullet" or sometimes a "torpedo" as a nickname for its long, cylindrical shape. The electric bullet smokers have a coil ring of heat in the bottom. The charcoal kind come with a charcoal chamber with a perforated ring that rests on top of the grill grate—all you have to do is pour a chimney starter of hot coals into the ring.

Most bullet smokers come with a water bowl, which rests inside the center station. Fill it with liquid—water, apple juice, or beer are all good choices. This liquid keeps a nice steam circulating inside the bullet to keep the meat from drying out *(see my water pan, page 51)*. Then close the door of your smoker and place the smaller, lower cooking grate inside the center station. Next, rest the larger upper cooking grate at the top of the center station. If you're using the charcoal kind, check the temperature every 20 minutes or so and shovel in hot coals as necessary to maintain your heat. If you're using the electric kind, you don't have to worry about shoveling coals. In both cases, you control the heat by opening and closing the vents as necessary.

OFFSET SMOKER

An **offset smoker** (also called an offset barrel smoker, a horizontal smoker, a pipe smoker, and a stick burner) is a charcoal smoker that has two parts: a cylindrical cooking chamber that is set horizontally (and not vertically, like the bullet) attached to a firebox, which has top or side door access and an adjustable vent. This design fairly well mimics a pit: The fire is built in one chamber and the smoke and heat surround the food in the other. This way the heat is next to (not under) the meat. A good offset smoker does not leak smoke through the doors; the connection between the firebox and the smoking chamber should be as airtight as possible (although no smoker is ever completely airtight)—many of them have doors and seams that seal tightly and so it's best to use those if you can.

Some have a convection plate, a perforated metal plate you can slide back and forth under the food in the smoke chamber to regulate airflow. Some have internal piping, baffles, and a chimney, which is also designed to regulate temperature evenly. To get to work, soak your wood chips overnight in water, then drain them when you're ready to cook. Begin with your vents open. Start your charcoal in a chimney starter and then spread them out over the rack at the bottom of the firebox. Use the vents to regulate the temperature. Put your meat on the grate in the cook chamber. Put your soaked wood on top of your burning coals in the firebox. Check your temp every 20 minutes, add new hot coals as necessary, and slide your vents to manage the heat.

CERAMIC SMOKER

A **ceramic smoker** was designed in homage to the Japanese cooking urns that have been popular in Asia for centuries. Some are made of terra cotta, cement, and even lava rock, which are thought to be excellent insulating materials and especially good at radiating and retaining heat; I've seen some do-it-yourself types build them out of larger flower pots. You can use ceramic cookers as pizza ovens and tandoori ovens for Indian food. You use these, essentially, by filling the bottom of the chamber up with charcoal—up to the bottom air holes. Start your fire with the bottom vent open, then sprinkle your presoaked wood chips on top of the fire. These smokers usually come with a perforated plate that rests over the charcoal chamber. A grate fits over the top of that. Close the smoker and open the vent in the lid. Let the smoker come to temperature. Then regulate your heat as you would with any other cooker, opening and closing the bottom and top vents as necessary.

H2O COOKER

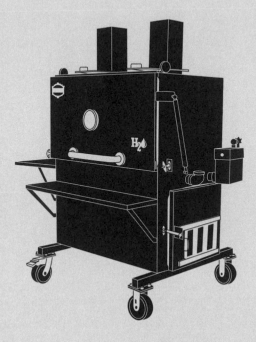

The **H2O Cooker** is what I use when I'm competing or whenever I'm smoking in a modern way. I have designed a whole line of these smokers—Myron Mixon Smokers (myronmixonsmokers.com)—that use a trademarked Waterpan Technology™, which uses an indirect water cooking system to evenly disperse heat throughout the cooking chamber and lock in the meat's natural juices while giving you the option of cooking hot and fast or low and slow. While I think our smokers are the best on the market, these types of water cookers are very popular with many of the best barbecue competition teams. Like most smokers, they are fueled by wood that provides smoke and heat. What makes these cookers special, though, is the water, which provides moisture, and the thick, insulated walls that keep the heat in. Whether you're cooking hot and fast or slow and low, these smokers allow you to cook three different ways at the same time: by smoking, roasting, and steaming. That allows you a lot of flexibility in how you can cook and the results can be amazing.

Now that we've got that out of the way

LET'S TALK THE TWO-STEP PROCESS

to get started with a smoker

STEP 1: SET UP THE WATER PAN

I like to use a water pan in the bottom of my smoker, and I get an awful lot of questions about it. Like everything else I do, it has a purpose, but this is a step you can certainly skip; using a water pan in your smoker is not a barbecue requirement, but I think it's a worthwhile enhancement. I happen to like it because it creates a water bath system inside the smoker that helps maintain the meat's moisture; it's like a maintenance device that helps keep some moisture in the smoker and helps tenderize the meat while you're barbecuing. Here's the method: Fill a heavy-bottomed medium pan (no bigger than a 13 x 9-inch / 33 x 23-cm lasagna pan) about halfway with water and clear an area in the middle of the bottom of your smoker to accommodate it, leaving coals stacked up on either side of the water pan.

STEP 2: LIGHT THE FIRE

When I start my smoker, I have never apologized for the fact that I like using lighter fluid to get a good blaze going and burn my wood—and let me be clear, I am what's known on the competition circuit as a "stick burner," which means I believe that nothing flavors meat better than whole sticks of wood and the natural smoke flavor that comes from burning them. I hate it when people say that if you use lighter fluid, the meat you cook will end up tasting like lighter fluid—that's only true if you don't know how to use it. After you apply the fluid, just let the coals burn for a while so the fluid burns off before you put your meat on to smoke.

HELPERS

The earliest pitmasters used what they had on hand. I'm talking about the first settlers to the American colonies who came from England. They had large families to feed and they had to feed them cheaply, so they fed them the livestock they had on the farms, they used the woods around them and the trees as their fuel, and they barbecued. And the way they barbecued is what we're going to do now—basically what we term "pit-fired" barbecue using masonry pits that are coal-fired—where we burn down the woods, make our coals, and shovel those coals into the pits to maintain a consistent temperature. And that's what they did. So when I say "meat helpers," I'm talking about the ingredients they used as far as flavoring.

When we talk about sauces, brines, and mops, they all have distilled vinegar as a base. Vinegar was used not only because it was a flavor additive but also because it was a preservative. The vinegar preserved the meat, kept it from going rank or bad. Our forefathers also had pepper flakes and salt, ingredients they kept down in the root cellar, and that's what they used for seasoning. It was very, very simple.

These early pitmasters were survivors, trying to make their way in this new country. And with pit barbecue they hit a home run right off the bat. The technique called barbecuing traveled all the way down the East Coast and into the South; this was before there was a Kansas City, before there was a Memphis, before people started migrating toward the Midwest, and before they came up with ketchup-based this and that and whatever. This is the way the majority of people on the East Coast barbecued, from Virginia all the way down through Georgia and Alabama. The flavors are vinegar based, the enhancers are red pepper flakes and salt, and that's what you had. And guess what? It's still a great combination of flavors today.

I'm going to give you two sauces: One is a vinegar-based sauce, a basic barbecue sauce you can use on anything, anytime, anywhere. The second one is a mustard-based sauce, which I'm including here because it's the sauce that my dad, Jack Mixon, made for my mom, who loved the pop and tang of mustard sauce. These two sauces are perfection, and I can't build on something better than that.

BARBECUE
SAUCES

Makes:

1 QUART (0.9 L)

MUSTARD-BASED

Mustard-based barbecue sauce is traditional in parts of South Carolina and Georgia—some historians think that's because these areas had a high population of German immigrants who came over in the 1700s and brought their tastes along with them. My mother happened to like mustard-based barbecue, and this is the sauce my daddy would whip up for her.

ingredients

2 cups (480 ml) distilled white vinegar

2 teaspoons freshly ground black pepper

2 teaspoons granulated sugar

2 teaspoons red pepper flakes

2 teaspoons ground chili powder

1 cup (220 g) packed dark brown sugar

2½ cups (600 ml) prepared yellow mustard

¼ cup (60 ml) ketchup

In a large heavy saucepan or stockpot, combine all the ingredients and whisk well. Cook over low heat for 20 minutes, whisking occasionally to combine. Do not bring the mixture to a boil. Let the sauce cool completely, about 30 minutes, then funnel it into a refrigerator-safe container. The sauce will keep, refrigerated, for up to a year.

VINEGAR-BASED

This is the basic formula for a classic vinegar sauce. You can add any or all of the following optional ingredients based on your personal flavor preferences: 1 cup (240 ml) ketchup, ½ cup (120 ml) hot sauce, ½ cup (100 g) sugar. Follow the exact same procedure, adding the extra ingredients to the pot with the others.

ingredients

1 quart (0.9 L) distilled white vinegar

1 tablespoon kosher salt

1 tablespoon coarsely ground black pepper

1 tablespoon red pepper flakes

In a large heavy saucepan or stockpot over medium heat, combine all the ingredients. Stir to dissolve the salt completely, cooking for 3 to 5 minutes of constant stirring. Do not bring the mixture to a boil. When the salt is thoroughly dissolved and the spices have infused the vinegar with their flavor, remove from the heat and let the sauce cool completely, about 30 minutes. Funnel the sauce into a refrigerator-safe container. The sauce will keep, refrigerated, for up to a year.

PIT BRINE

A brine is a solution of salt and water; if you soak meat in it before cooking, it will tenderize it and keep it from drying out, which is a danger in all cooking but especially in pit smoking. Brining enhances juiciness and moisture when you submerge your meat in the solution. Here I'm giving you a recipe for basic brine that I like for pit smoking in particular, where fancy flavors are not necessary. If you want to add some other ingredients in here, like your favorite herbs and spices, that's fine. I don't, because for me cooking old-school barbecue isn't about trying to make something that you'd find in a damn French restaurant; we're talking about the basics here, how barbecue got started.

Makes:

ABOUT 3 GALLONS (11.4 L)

ingredients

3 cups (720 g) kosher salt

3 cups (600 g) sugar

In a large heavy stockpot over high heat, bring 3 gallons (11.4 L) water to a boil. Add the salt and sugar and stir until dissolved. Remove from the heat and let cool completely, about 30 minutes. If reserving for later use, funnel the brine into a container and store in the refrigerator for up to 2 weeks.

PIT MOP

A mop is basically a meat-moistening agent, and its main ingredient is vinegar *(see page 53 for the importance of vinegar to barbecue)*. The mop also infuses a little flavor into the meat, an added layer of complexity. We mop almost all of our long-cooking meats at varying intervals dependent on how many pounds of meat we're dealing with—each recipe has a specific time at which to open the pit and mop, ranging from every fifteen minutes to every thirty after a meat's "crust" forms. Mopping is especially important in smoking because we're cooking with actual coals beneath the meat, and we don't want our meat to dry out.

Makes:

ABOUT 1 ½ GALLONS (5.7 L)

ingredients

1 gallon (3.8 L) distilled white vinegar

½ cup (40 g) red pepper flakes

½ cup (120 g) kosher salt

4 lemons, cut in half

Combine all the ingredients and ½ gallon (1.9 L) water in a large pot over medium-high heat. Bring to a boil, and let the pepper flakes open up and the pepper seeds open out into the liquid and give it some seasoning. Let the mop cool completely, about 1 hour, then funnel it into a container large enough to hold it. It will keep for year in the refrigerator, and you can portion it out as you cook your barbecue along the way.

To apply the mop to the meat, take a brand-new floor mop, cutting the handle to a size short enough so that it's easy for you to manipulate, and periodically use it to dab the liquid mop onto the meat to give it moisture and also to give it flavor, that southern-style barbecue flavor that a mop's all about.

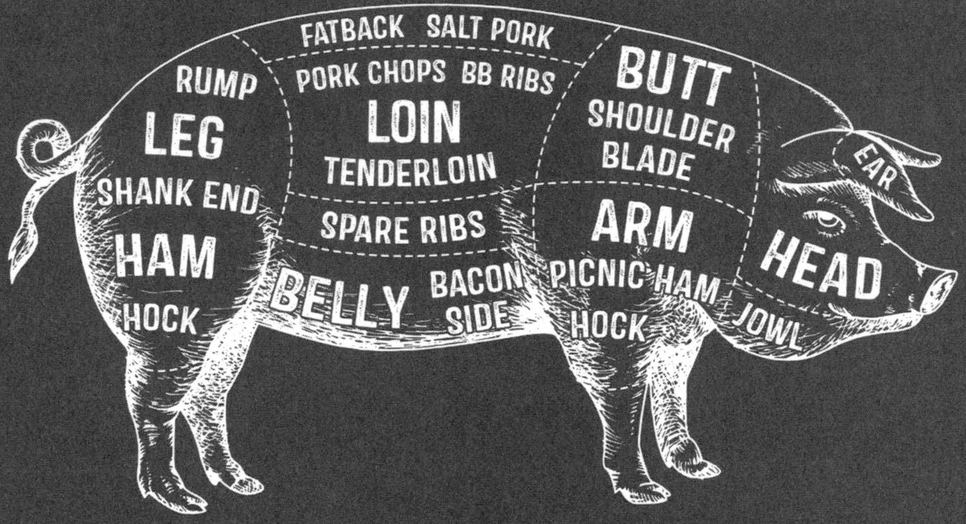
FATBACK
SALT PORK
RUMP
PORK CHOPS
BB RIBS
BUTT
LEG
LOIN
SHOULDER
BLADE
TENDERLOIN
EAR
SHANK END
SPARE RIBS
ARM
HAM
HEAD
BELLY
BACON
SIDE
PICNIC HAM
HOCK
HOCK
JOWL

CHAPTER 2:
the
HOG

WHOLE HOG

The very best reason to consider making a whole hog is because you're fixin' to have a whole lot of people over to your house for someone's birthday or an engagement celebration, or because it's the Fourth of July (come to think of it, that's a birthday party, too). Remember when I said that barbecue is a social food? (You can refresh yourself by turning to *page 25*.) Well, the whole hog is the most social entrée in the field. To me a pig pickin' is the ultimate expression of our southern culture, because it's the time when friends and family get together over a meal to share stories and make memories; it's the ritual that bonds us. I'm not going to pretend with you: Making a whole hog is something that requires effort and patience. But when you master it, it's like mastering any other craft because you acquire knowledge that will last you a lifetime. In this case, you also have something uniquely delicious to show for it. Come on, I'll teach you.

COAL-FIRED
PIT-SMOKED
WHOLE HOG

Whole hog was something my dad didn't cook a lot of: He liked to do the joint meats more, the hams and shoulders. He did whole hogs as special requests, or when he wanted to show off a little bit at Christmastime when he had all the family over.

Remember when I told you about how my dad never used meat thermometers or gauges? (If you don't, turn to *page 42* and see how he ran his hand on top of a sheet of tin and counted to ten.) Learning to test meat for doneness without the aid of a thermometer is one of the marks of an experienced pitmaster. The ability to do it comes with time and repetition. You will make some mistakes along the way, but mastering the ability to test meat for doneness will give you a whole lot of confidence in your barbecue and certainly take away a lot of stress. When it comes to the whole hog, it's like your personal learning laboratory: Pay attention to the way different meats on the hog look when it's ready to be pulled from the pit.

Cooking time:	Makes:
10 TO 12 HOURS	**20 TO 25 SERVINGS**

for the hog

1 (160-pound / 73-kg) hog, head-on, butterflied

1 quart (0.9 L) distilled white vinegar

1 gallon (3.8 L) Pit Mop (page 57)

Vinegar-Based Barbecue Sauce (page 55)

1 cup (240 g) kosher salt

1 cup (96 g) coarsely ground black pepper

1: SELECT AND PREP THE MEAT

Daddy always liked to get an old breed of pork, a Duroc or a Hampshire or a cross between the two. These are old breeds that came over in the early 1800s; they're very red-meated hogs with a high marbling content and a lot of flavor, and you know that's where it's at. (Other good old American domestic hog breeds to consider are the Berkshire and the Yorkshire. These old breeds are making a comeback; you can ask any butcher to order one of these for you.) The hogs he selected would have marbling all the way down through the meat: I ain't just talking about the fat on the outside of the hog when he split it open, I'm talking about the marbling running down the side of it. He liked to use about a 160-pound (73-kg) hog with the head on; he'd have him what we call "butterflied," where the belly is actually split right down the middle and the hog will lay flat out. Again, a butcher can do this for you.

There's not a lot of prep involved. The first thing you need to do is make a prep area: On a long table covered with clean butcher paper or another sanitary covering, lay your hog on its back with its cavity facing up. Next Jack would go in and remove the feet, and then he'd remove all the fat that was inside the cavity that he could pull away with his hands; you will ask your butcher to do those things for you. Then he'd take white vinegar and rub it all over the inside of the cavity, touching any exposed meat. There are a couple of reasons for this: One is because of that flavor profile we all associate with barbecue in the South—vinegar, vinegar sauce, and vinegar-based pork. Another is that vinegar is a disinfectant that kills bacteria that might have gotten on the hog. Finally, the vinegar wet the inside of the hog where he was going to apply his seasoning, which was just salt and pepper. He also applied it all over the outside, on the skin, too.

2: MAKE THE GURNEY

Most of the cookers you see these days don't require you to flip the hog; it cooks in the exact position in which you lay it in there. In pit-fired barbecue, the meat has to be flipped. The way you do that with a 160-pound (73-kg) piece of meat is to prepare it first, and then mount it on a gurney. So what my dad did, like everybody before him, was make a "hog gurney" in order to handle the whole animal. Here's how to make one:

1. Lay one piece of fencing out on a table, then pick the hog up and put him belly down onto the wire. Then lay the second piece of fencing directly on top of the hog in line with the sheet beneath the hog.

for the gurney

2 to 3 x 6-foot (0.6 to 0.9 x 1.8-m) welded wire fence, cut to fit the hog (hardware or home improvement stores can cut it for you)

3 feet (0.9 m) aluminum wire, for fastening

2 black pipes a bit longer than the length of the hog (4 to 5 feet / 1.2 to 1.5 m), ½ inch (12 mm) thick

Fencing pliers

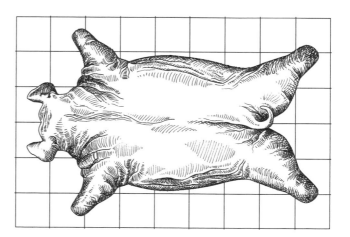

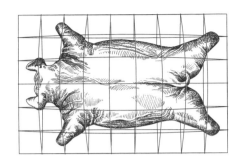

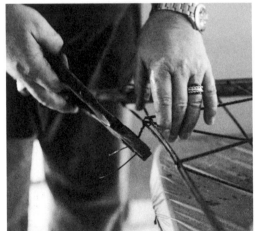

2. Wire the fencing together all the way down both sides of the hog.

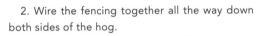

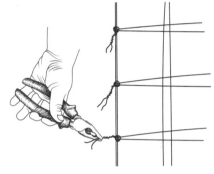

3. Take the two pieces of black pipe and run them down each side of the fencing. Wire the pipe to the fencing to secure each side, and now you've got a gurney.

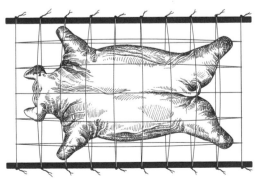

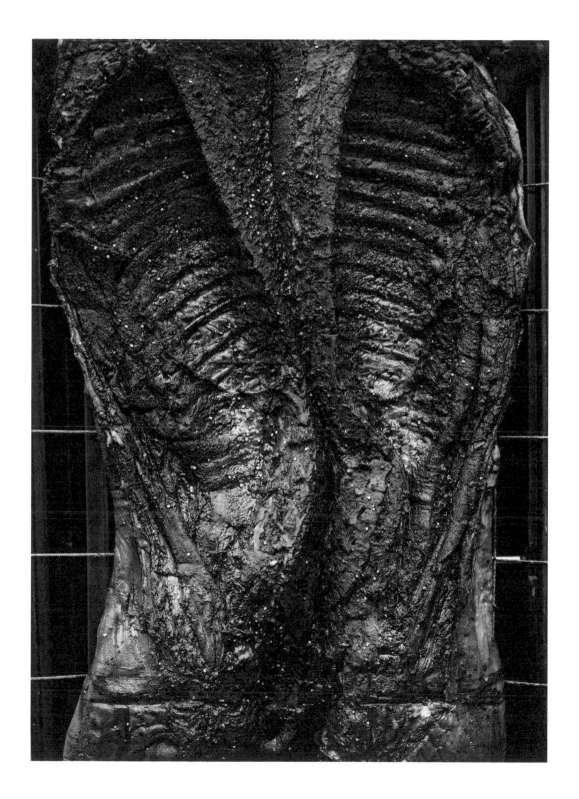

3: PREPARE THE PIT OR SMOKER AND PUT THE MEAT ON *(see pages 41-51 for details)*

My dad liked to use a ratio of 3:1 in his combination of woods in his burn barrel to make coals. He'd use three sticks of green red oak (green being fresh cut) to one stick of green hickory. He'd start his fire early in the morning because it takes 3 to 4 hours to get a good bucket of coals burning out of your burn barrel. Once that happened, he'd fire the pits and start getting the pits up to temp, to about 250°F (120°C). (If you put the meat on first and then start firing your pits, you're prolonging the cooking process.) So we'd get the pits fired, get the masonry up to temp, and then we'd put the hog, belly down in the gurney, on top of the grate in the pit.

It takes about 2 hours until you can actually hear the dripping fat hitting the coals beneath it and then steaming and sizzling back up. That is a big part of the flavor profile of this style of cooking: Where that meat and fat is rendering, it drops that fat down onto those coals below, hits the coals, and steams back up and hits the meat, providing a unique flavor profile that you can't get any other way.

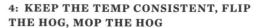

4: KEEP THE TEMP CONSISTENT, FLIP THE HOG, MOP THE HOG

This hog is cooking, rendering and dripping fat, and I wish we had dang scratch 'n' sniff for this book because that smell is unique to this style of cooking and like no other you'll ever smell. We'll cook this hog for about 6 hours, all the while shoveling the coals, keeping that temperature around 250 to 275°F (120 to 135°C), and you just hear the meat sizzling in there and hear the dripping, hear the coals steaming and giving the meat that flavor that we're looking for. And at that 6-hour mark, we'll go in with our leather gloves, and with two people, we'll grab the ends of the gurney by the pipe, then flip it on its back. We've got a crust built up inside that cavity now, and we'll need to take our mop *(see page 57)* and apply it all over the hog, and in that cavity. Now we put the lid back down and keep the pits fired. About every hour and a half, Daddy would pull the tin back and we'd go in and do another mop, all down inside the cavity and over the skin.

5: TEST FOR DONENESS

Now we're getting to our 10-hour mark, and we start checking this meat for doneness. My daddy did this by grabbing the leg bones and the rib bones to see how they're pulling and if they're getting tender. You want it almost falling-off-the-bone tender. If the bones are slipping easily, we're going to pull the hog out; if not, we're going on that 12-hour mark. And again we're mopping about every hour, hour and a half, with our vinegar mop.

6: PULL AND EAT THAT MEAT

Once it's done, put on your heavy-duty work gloves and then pull the tin back, pull the hog out, and put it on the picnic table. Cut the fencing loose. If we were having a pig picking, Daddy would pull the spine out, pull the rib bones back, and then apply some vinegar-based sauce *(see page 55)*, and that's what you should do, too: Get your heavy-duty gloves on and pull the spine out of your way (discard it), pull the ribs aside, and you'll have a whole bunch of meat facing you. The meat now has got a flavor that's out of this world, and you've also got the skin. The skin now's like cracklings, with crispy edges that you can just break off and enjoy as a tasty on-the-spot treat right there.

IN THE SMOKER

I sincerely want everyone to try the unique coal-fired pitmaster whole hog, and I've made it as simple for you as I can (remember, for less than $400 you can build the whole pit yourself; see page 38*). However, for a down-and-dirty easy method of smoking a whole hog in an industrial-size smoker, here you go:*

PREP:

Start with your 160-pound (73-kg) hog, butterflied and with extra fat removed for you by your butcher. On a long table covered with clean butcher paper or another sanitary covering, lay long strips of aluminum foil. Lay the hog flat on its back on top of the foil. Apply white vinegar, salt, and pepper all over the hog, inside and out, including on the skin, taking care to sprinkle the salt and pepper throughout the cavity and on the surface of any exposed meat. Gather up the foil you've laid the hog on and use it to loosely wrap the entire hog. Let the hog rest this way for 1 hour while you light the smoker and bring it to 250°F (120°C).

COOK:

Place the hog in the smoker. Close the smoker and let the hog smoke for about 20 hours, or until the internal temperature of the meatiest part of the shoulder is 205°F (95°C). (I often set my hog on the smoker at noon the day before I want to eat it; then I remove it at 8:00 the next morning and let it rest until I'm ready to eat.) Unwrap the foil and, using a brush, apply a mop you've made of white vinegar, salt, and red pepper flakes throughout the inside of the cavity. Rewrap the hog loosely in the foil. Leaving the hog in the smoker, let the temperature fall from 250°F

(120°C) until the hog is cool enough to handle and remove from the pit (no more wood is needed at this point). This resting allows the hog meat to redistribute its juice and for the meat to cool down just enough so that folks can start pulling the meat without getting hurt.

EAT:

Unless you need to present the whole hog, the hog is left in the smoker while it is picked and pulled and, best of all, eaten. In true southern tradition, the hog is never "carved," per se. Wearing clean heavy-duty gloves and using either large tongs or your hands, gently pull the meat out of the hog in chunks and pile it onto large trays or straight onto plates.

GROWING UP *with* JACK MIXON

M Y DADDY ALWAYS made my brother, Tracy, and me help him cook the food for his barbecue restaurant. It was a carryout place, open only on Thursdays, Fridays, and Saturdays—but only on Saturdays if there was any meat leftover and he hadn't sold out before then. Most of the time he wore what he always wore: a white T-shirt with the sleeves cut off, a pair of damn suspenders holding up his jeans, his work boots, and his truck driver's cap. He'd sit on this five-gallon bucket he'd turn upside down and watch us shovel coals into the pits, and then every so often he'd get up and run his hand over the sheet of tin that covered the pits and check to make sure the temperature inside them was consistent.

At that time in my life, I hated barbecue; it was hard work, especially turning on one of them gas grills. All I could think about in my younger days was when I was going to be able to get away from there, to get the hell out of that mess. Little did I know it, but I was learning the whole time. You can probably call my dad's style "tough love." Under that kind of love you either get stronger or you break down. I know that if he hadn't made us learn how to become pitmasters, we wouldn't have. Tracy didn't pick it up like I did; he was younger than me. But he also had it easier: As the oldest, I came under the harshest guns of Jack. My brother got to go hang out with his friends but I didn't, and if I bitched about it I got in serious trouble. When my mom passed away and Tracy started working with me, he learned the things he never learned from Daddy. I don't think that Jack didn't want Tracy to learn it, I just think I brought out the worst in my dad somehow; the bright side of that is the fact that I learned the most from him—probably because I was most like him.

Sometimes to this day Tracy misspeaks and calls me "Daddy" when I'm arguing with him about something. In truth my dad had to have us work for him because we had to have the money; most of the time he couldn't afford to hire labor. I remember one time we had a sawmill where we custom-cut cypress that we logged out of the swamps, and we hired a cutting crew to turn it into lumber. We had a yard full of timber and we custom-cut it for decking and stuff like that. We probably had twelve people working with us; I was about fourteen or fifteen years old. We were squaring up the logs and it was so messy; cypress wood is full of water, and the sawdust comes off wet and sticks to you like cornmeal. One day I told Tracy, "We're working as hard as people in the world, and we ought to get paid." That night while we were sitting at the dinner table, I was full of vinegar and feeling like I was grown-up and ought to be treated like it. I told my dad I thought we ought to get paid. He said, "You sit your ass at my table, you eat the food I buy, you wear the clothes I buy you, you sleep under my roof, you are getting paid." And that was the end of that. My momma was sensitive, and Tracy is too. My momma always said they ought to saint her for putting up with Jack. With him, everything was either black or white; there wasn't any gray.

Now, my daddy didn't sweat the big stuff, but something small would happen and he could get off on a tangent. You could do something that was a major screwup and he'd be OK, but if you did something little he could lose it. Nevertheless, he was beloved. In a county of 10,000 people, about 1,000 came to my daddy's funeral, including the local law enforcement who loved him. He knew a lot of people; he was a great athlete when he was in high school, and to the end he was charismatic. Daddy would not believe the damn notoriety of where barbecue is today. For southerners like him, barbecue was just a way of life. Right now in this country southern stuff is cool and everyone wants to get something that's supposedly southern, which he wouldn't understand, either. My dad thought "southern" meant working your ass off and getting by, and there was nothing wrong with that.

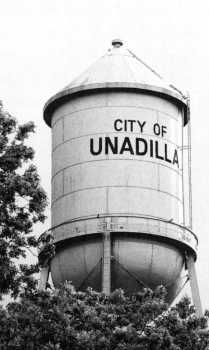

HOG PARTS

I'm not going to lie to you: The whole hog is easily the Mount Everest of barbecue, the biggest, baddest challenge out there. It is much easier to cook the hog parts separately simply because they're easier to handle when they're smaller, from managing their prep to monitoring their cook times. You might consider these "hog parts" the building blocks of whole-hog cooking, or simply the meats to cook for smaller occasions. I've thrown a couple of personal favorite recipes in here for cooking some cuts of hog that are a bit more unusual, too, such as the snout and the tail. Big-city chefs and restaurateurs may brag about "nose-to-tail" cooking, but southern barbecue guys like me have been cooking all the parts of the hog worth eating since before there was a borough called Brooklyn (by about fifty years, in fact).

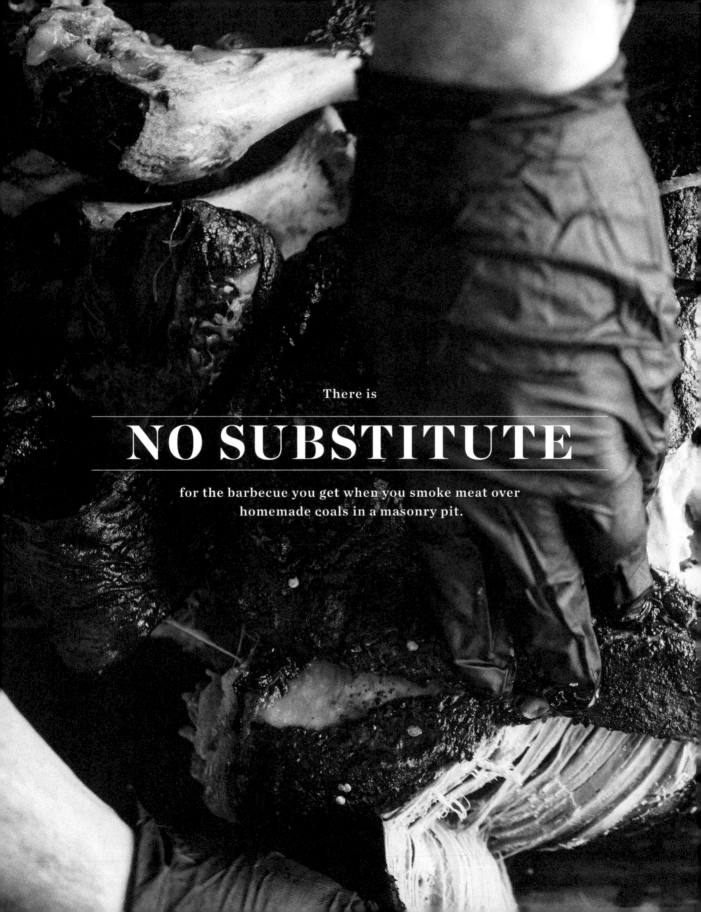

There is

NO SUBSTITUTE

for the barbecue you get when you smoke meat over
homemade coals in a masonry pit.

SMOKED
SHOULDER

It will generally take about the same amount of time to cook a couple of pork shoulders as it will to cook the whole hog. The reason for that: When you look at a whole hog to determine the length of time you'll have to cook it, you're looking at the size of the biggest pieces of meat on there, and that will be the shoulders (and hams). Because these shoulders are about the same size as the ones on the whole hog, you're looking at 10 to 12 hours here.

Cooking time:	Makes:
10 TO 12 HOURS	**25 TO 30 SERVINGS**

ingredients

1 (15- to 20-pound / 6.8- to 9-kg) bone-in whole pork shoulder

Distilled white vinegar

Kosher salt and freshly ground black pepper

Pit Mop *(page 57)*

Vinegar-Based Barbecue Sauce *(page 55)*

1: SELECT AND PREP THE MEAT

Daddy didn't trim pork shoulders too much—maybe he cut away extra skin or large hunks of sinew hanging off a shoulder, but mostly he kept it simple and liked to take the shoulders straight from the butcher, lay them out on a table covered with butcher paper or another sanitary covering, and rub them down all over the inside and the outside with white vinegar. Then we'd season them all over with salt and pepper.

2: PREPARE THE PIT OR SMOKER AND PUT THE MEAT ON *(see pages 41-51 for details)*

Place the shoulder in the pit, meat side down, and then start shoveling your coals underneath.

3: KEEP THE TEMP CONSISTENT, FLIP AND MOP THE SHOULDER

We'll cook the shoulders for about 6 hours, all the while shoveling the coals, keeping that temperature around the 250°F (120°C) mark so you hear the meat sizzling and its juices dripping and hear the coals steaming and giving the meat that flavor we're looking for. After 6 hours we'll go in with our leather gloves and flip the shoulders. My dad would take his Case pocketknife and he'd poke about three holes in the skin on the shoulder and then we'd flip it skin side down. So use a sharp knife to poke three holes in the skin, flip the shoulder, place it back on the grate over the coals skin side down, and let the liquid run out and hit the coals and steam up on the meat.

When we flip the shoulders at the 6-hour mark we're going to take that mop we made and dab that mop all over the shoulders, even on the skin. Now we put the lid back down. Now we keep firing again. About every hour and a half, we pull the tin back, we go in and do another mop, and we close it.

4: TEST FOR DONENESS

When we get to our 10-hour mark, we start checking the meat for doneness. My dad did this by grabbing the blade bone and pulling it. (You can wear your heavy-duty work gloves to do this if you like.) You want that meat almost falling-off-the-bone tender. If the bones are slipping easily, we're going to pull the shoulders out; if not, we're going on that 12-hour mark. Again we're mopping about every hour and a half.

5: PULL AND EAT THAT MEAT

My dad pulled all the meat from the shoulders by hand and with tongs, simply grabbing off pieces and collecting them in a large aluminum pan, and then we'd lightly sauce the meat with a vinegar-based sauce right there and make barbecue platters or sandwiches, or we'd process the meat for Brunswick Stew *(page 103)* or a catering job. You'll notice you've got a lot of skin left over, which is perfect for making cracklin's *(page 102)*.

IN THE SMOKER

Here's a down-and-dirty easy method to smoke a shoulder on a smoker:

PREP:

Start with one 15- to 20-pound (6.8- to 9-kg) pork shoulder. Rub it down thoroughly with white vinegar and season it liberally with salt and pepper, taking care to cover all surfaces. Prepare a smoker with soaked wood chips *(see page 44)* and heat it to 250°F (120°C).

COOK:

Place the shoulder directly on the smoker rack. Cook for 3 hours, then transfer it into a clean aluminum pan and cover with foil. Place the pan back on the smoker and finish cooking the shoulder until the internal temperature reaches 205°F (95°C). Pull the pan from the smoker and let the shoulder rest while still covered for at least 2 hours.

EAT:

Put on clean heavy-duty gloves and pull the meat apart in chunks. Discard the gloves and, using tongs, toss the meat with a vinegar-based barbecue sauce, if you like. Pile the pulled pork on guests' plates or sandwich buns.

Keeping Meat Moist the Jack Mixon Way

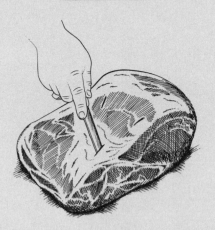

I was always reluctant to ask my daddy why he was doing something, because he might tear my ass up if I did. The two words he hated to hear out of his young'uns were "Why?" and "What?" He'd rather you watch him do something and figure it out on your own. By the time I had the courage to ask him why he poked those three holes in the pork shoulder, I was in my late twenties. He said, "I poke them holes in that meat for two reasons: First reason is that when I flip it over on the skin, all that liquid that's in there—the grease and water and everything that's been rendering out while it's been cooking with the meat side down—is going to run out and hit those coals and have more of a steaming effect, steaming back up on that meat, which is a big part of the flavor. Second thing is, when I get that liquid away from it, it's going to cook faster and get done sooner." When I asked if doing it that way would dry the shoulders out, he looked at me and said, "Have you ever eaten any of my barbecue that was dried out?" And I said, "No, sir." And that ended that conversation.

SMOKED
SPARERIBS

Spareribs, or St. Louis–style ribs as they're known on the professional barbecue circuit, are the ribs of choice down here in the Deep South; people raised in our area want the biggest bang for their buck, so we like spareribs, which are surrounded by more fat to flavor the meat than, say, a baby back or a trimmed-up Kansas City–style rib (the latter is the St. Louis rib minus the top part of the bone so that the rack has ribs uniformly square in size). These are what we cooked when I was growing up. We cooked big spares, and my dad never even removed the membrane or trimmed them up too much, either.

Cooking time:	Serves:
4 TO 6 HOURS	**8 TO 12**

ingredients

4 racks spareribs

Distilled white vinegar

Kosher salt and freshly ground black pepper

Pit Mop *(page 57)*

Vinegar-Based Barbecue Sauce *(page 55)*

1: SELECT AND PREP THE MEAT

We're going to use four racks of whole large spareribs, not separated into individual ribs. We're going to place each rack one at a time on a cutting board, bone side down, and use a sharp knife to trim off any excess fat from the first three ribs. We're going to turn the slab over, make a small incision just below the length of the breastbone, work our fingers underneath the thick membrane

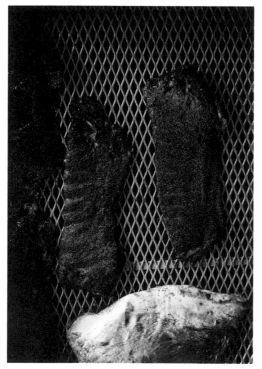

(called "silver"), and firmly peel off that thick membrane that covers the ribs. Sometimes this exposes more fat that needs trimming, so trim that away if it's there. Now we're going to go in with white vinegar and dab the ribs all over with it. Then we're going to season the ribs well on both sides with salt and pepper.

2: PREPARE THE PIT OR SMOKER AND PUT THE MEAT ON (see pages 41-51 for details)

Bring the temperature to 265°F (130°C). Place the racks of ribs in the pit, meat side down, and then start shoveling your coals underneath.

3: KEEP THE TEMP CONSISTENT, FLIP AND MOP THE RIBS

After 2 hours, we're coming into the pit with long, heavy tongs to flip the racks so the bones go down onto the bricks. We're going to mop all over both sides of our ribs. We're going to mop every 30 minutes until we get to the 4-hour mark and then check for doneness. With ribs, you need to be very careful about mopping because the more time you have that tin pulled back, the more oxygen is getting down in there to those smoldering coals, and the more apt you are to have flame-ups. You get the tin up, you mop all the meat, you pull the tin back down, and be done with it. It takes me about 30 seconds.

4: TEST FOR DONENESS

When we get to our 4-hour mark, we start checking the meat for doneness. My dad did this by grabbing the rib bones and pulling at them. You can do this with heavy-duty gloves on if you like, but it's easier to pull the rib without them. You want that meat almost falling-off-the-bone tender. If the bones slip easily, we're going to pull the ribs out; if not, we're going on that 6-hour mark and will keep mopping them every 30 minutes.

5: PULL AND EAT THAT MEAT

We pull the ribs off and lightly sauce the racks by brushing all over on both sides with our vinegar sauce. The crispy "bark" on the outside of the ribs, where the fat has been rendering out perfectly, is so damn good. Using heavy kitchen shears or a sharp knife, cut the ribs to separate them, then serve.

IN THE SMOKER

Here's a down-and-dirty easy method to smoke ribs in a smoker:

PREP:

Start with 4 racks of spareribs. Rub them down thoroughly with white vinegar, then season them all over with salt and pepper. Set the racks in an aluminum baking pan and let sit uncovered at room temperature for about 30 minutes.

COOK:

Prepare a smoker with soaked wood chips and heat it to 275°F (135°C). Remove the ribs from the pan and place them directly on the smoker grate. After 2 hours, transfer the ribs to a clean large aluminum pan, bone side down. Pour 1 cup of water into the pan with the ribs and then cover the pan with foil. Place the pan back on the smoker and finish cooking the ribs for 2 more hours, or until tender. When the ribs are tender, remove the pan from the smoker, brush the ribs with vinegar-based barbecue sauce *(page 55)*, and transfer them back to the smoker (no pan) for 10 minutes for the sauce to set.

EAT:

Remove the ribs from the smoker and let them rest for 10 minutes, uncovered, on a wooden cutting board. Cut the ribs to separate them and serve.

Smoked Pig Tails
and Trotters

These are smoked in a pit that's already fired up to 250 to 275°F (120 to 135°C)—when you're already cooking something else, most likely a whole hog, or hams or chickens. If you opt to cook a whole hog, you'll already have a tail, four trotters, and a snout to work with; if you don't, any butcher can get you trotters, tails, and snouts (or "SNOOT," as we pronounce it down here in south Georgia; see *page 100* for my Smoked Snout Sandwich recipe). These are very inexpensive parts that tend to make some folks squeamish, but I'm here to tell you that they're well worth cooking, because when they're done right, they make for very, very good eating indeed.

SMOKED PIG TAILS

Pig tails should come from a large hog because they've got more meat and fat on them, making for better cooking and eating. To prepare the pig tails, rinse them thoroughly in cold water and pat them dry completely with a clean kitchen towel or paper towels. Spritz or brush the tails with distilled white vinegar and season them all over with salt and pepper. Then put them in the pit right there along with the rest of the meats you're cooking.

Cook the pig tails for 1½ hours. Then roll them over onto the uncooked side and cook them for another 1½ hours. You're looking for a crispy exterior here, and 3 hours of cooking time is going to do that for you. Now transfer the tails to a heavy cast-iron skillet or another heavy-duty pan. Pour a mop made of distilled white vinegar and crushed red pepper into the pan so that the mop comes about three-quarters of the way up the sides of the tails. Put the skillet in the pit and cook until the tails are tender and falling off the bone, about 2 more hours. Serve with plenty of sauce *(page 55)* on the side for dipping and homemade potato salad.

SMOKED TROTTERS

The process for trotters is very similar to the process for pig tails. To prep the trotters, split each one lengthwise straight down the middle, so that you have two halves (you can have your butcher split them for you).

Clean them very well, rinsing thoroughly in cold water and patting them dry completely with a clean kitchen towel or paper towels. Apply distilled white vinegar to both sides of each piece, which you can do with a spritz bottle or a brush.

Season the pieces well on both sides with salt and pepper.

Meanwhile, you've got your pit at 250 to 275°F (120 to 135°C) and you're shoveling and checking the temperature and taking care to maintain it. Put the trotters in the pit, cut side down, on the grate. Cook them like this for 2 hours.

Flip them skin side down and cook for another 2 hours. Now get a good heavy cast-iron skillet or other heavy-duty pan and transfer your trotters into it.

Pour a mop made of distilled white vinegar and crushed red pepper into the pan so that the mop comes about three-quarters of the way up the sides of the trotters.

Put the skillet into the pit and cook the trotters for about 2 more hours in the pan, just leaving them in the pan while you're still firing the pit. What this is going to do is tenderize that meat to where it's going to be falling-off-the-bone tender, where you can pick up a trotter and you can gnaw down on it and you can get between every bone in there. I don't care if this sounds a little primal; that's some good eating.

SMOKED
WHOLE HAM

If you've followed my method for the whole hog and the hog shoulders, you should see a pattern: same technique, different cut. A fresh ham is my favorite and was my daddy's favorite meat to cook. He liked white meat and he liked the fact that with hams you don't have a lot of fat and so you get a high yield—good for his barbecue business. (The shoulder, on the other hand, is full of marbling and fat, so when you cook it you end up with significantly less volume than you started with.) In his signature barbecue, my dad liked to combine pulled pork shoulder meat with pulled ham in a ratio of 1:3, shoulder to ham. He'd take one cooked shoulder and three cooked hams, blend all of that meat together, lightly sauce it with that vinegar-based sauce, and serve it. That meat he sold for take-out was a big part of his business, and it was a winning formula. Or you can just enjoy your smoked hams and the best chopped or sliced ham sandwiches you'll ever eat.

Cooking time:	Makes:
10 TO 12 HOURS	**ABOUT 25 SERVINGS**

ingredients

1 (18- to 22-pound / 8.2- to 10-kg) fresh ham with the skin on

Distilled white vinegar

Kosher salt and freshly ground black pepper

Pit Mop (page 57)

Vinegar-Based Barbecue Sauce (page 55)

1: SELECT AND PREP THE MEAT

We don't trim the ham, but we prep it by rubbing it down, skin and all, with white vinegar, then applying salt and pepper all over the skin and the meat. This is very easy.

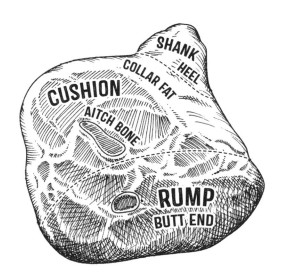

IN THE SMOKER

Here's a down-and-dirty easy method to smoke a ham in a smoker:

PREP:

Start with 1 (15-pound / 6.8-kg) precooked smoked ham on the bone. Prepare a smoker with soaked wood chips and heat it to 225°F (110°C). Trim the tough outer skin and excess fat from the ham.

COOK:

Place the ham meat side down on the rack in the smoker and smoke the ham for 3 hours. Transfer the ham from the smoker into a large clean aluminum pan, cover the pan with foil, and put the pan back on the smoker. Finish cooking the ham for 2 more hours, covered, in the pan. Remove the pan from the smoker and let the ham rest, covered, for at least 2 hours.

MOP:

Take the ham off the smoker. Apply a favorite glaze or barbecue sauce to the ham with a brush, covering it all over. Put the ham back in the aluminum pan, cover it with foil, and return it to the smoker. Smoke the ham for about 1 hour more, or until the internal temperature is right around 145°F (65°C). Unwrap the foil and baste the ham again with your favorite glaze or barbecue sauce. Cover the ham again, return it to the smoker, and smoke for about 1 hour more. At this point the ham will be at least 145°F (65°C), possibly a little higher.

EAT:

Remove the ham from the smoker, loosely tent it with fresh foil, and allow it to rest for 30 minutes. Carve and serve warm or at room temperature, or follow the directions in step 5 on *page 83* for pulled pork.

2: PREPARE THE PIT OR SMOKER AND PUT THE MEAT ON *(see pages 41–51 for details)*

Bring the temperature to 265°F (130°C). Place the ham in the pit, meat side down, and then start shoveling your coals underneath.

3: KEEP THE TEMP CONSISTENT, FLIP AND MOP THE HAM

At the 6-hour mark, poke three holes in the back of the ham, flip it, and let the accumulated juices run out onto the coals so the liquid steams back up onto the meat. Then we're going to take that pit mop and dab mop all over the ham, even the skin. We're going to mop the ham thoroughly every hour after the 6-hour mark until the 9-hour mark, when we'll test for doneness.

4: TEST FOR DONENESS

Now that we're getting to our 9-hour mark, we start checking this meat for doneness. My dad did this by grabbing the leg bone and pulling it. You want that meat almost falling-off-the-bone tender. If the bone is slipping easily, we're going to pull the ham out; if not, we're going on that 10-hour mark.

5: PULL AND EAT THAT MEAT

Transfer the cooked ham to a cutting board. Cover loosely with foil and let rest for 20 minutes. Pull off any crisp skin and, if you're so inclined, finely chop it with a cleaver. Wearing clean heavy-duty gloves, pull the meat off the bones in large pieces; discard any bones or lumps of fat. Using your fingers or a couple of forks, pull each piece of pork into thin shreds, or finely chop with a cleaver. Transfer the pork to a large, heatproof pan and stir in about 2½ cups (600 ml) of the barbecue sauce, enough to keep the meat moist; add more as needed. Season the pork with salt and pepper. Then pile it up on buns.

If you ride through

SOUTH GEORGIA

right now, in 90 percent of the yards you drive past there will be some sort
of smoker or grill or pit—that's the way we were raised down here.

HOG EXTRAS

I don't like the term "leftovers" for a whole bunch of reasons, not least because it sounds like an insult. What I do like is the concept of saving what you don't eat and repurposing it for future use, and also the concept of using what you've cooked on the pit or in the smoker in unexpected ways—both of those techniques keep life interesting, don't they? My "hog extras," as I like to call them, give you a good idea of how I might use a couple of pounds of pulled pork after I'm sick of sandwiches, or what I do with all the hog skin after a pig pickin', or even, yes, how I might enjoy the nose of the beast (that's one delicious sandwich—try it).

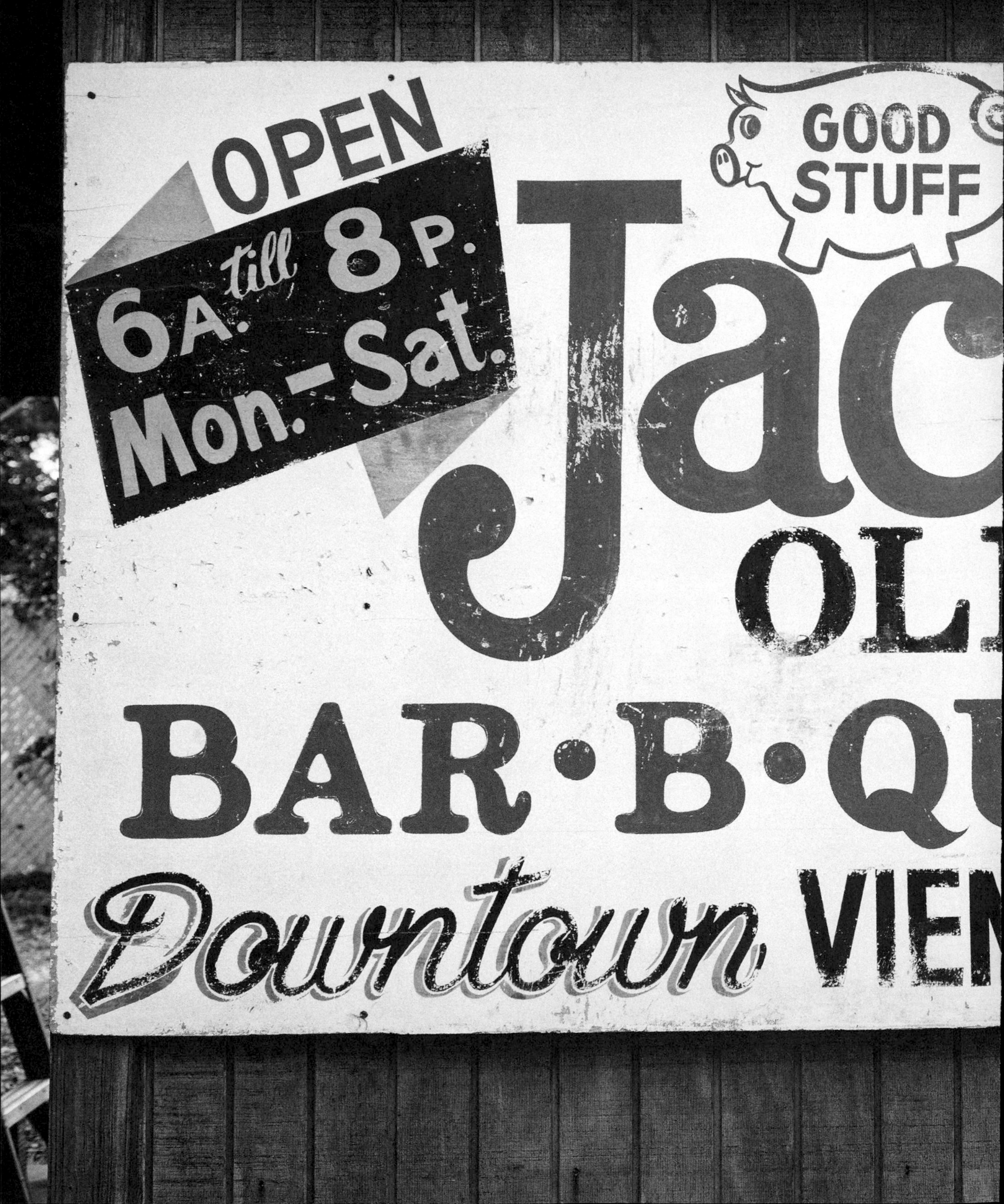
OPEN
6A. till 8P.
Mon.-Sat.
GOOD
STUFF
Jac
OL
BAR·B·Q
Downtown VIE

K'S

D SOUTH
E & GRILL
NA

SMOKED
SNOUT
SANDWICH

In South Georgia we call a pig's snout a "snoot" or a "rooter" (because it's what a hog uses to root around for acorns). If you buy these from the butcher, the snout will include the top part of the hog's nose, with the skin on it and the nostril holes in it. The goal in cooking these is to make them very crispy, so you don't want to cook them the same way as the trotters and the pig tails. It's also important to note that you eat them in sandwich form, and to have in mind that you're making them almost like you would make cracklin's *(page 102)*.

Makes:

1 SANDWICH

ingredients

1 pig snout

Pit Mop *(page 57)*

Kosher salt and freshly ground black pepper

Bread of choice

Vinegar-Based Barbecue Sauce *(page 55; optional)*

Dill pickles, sliced *(optional)*

Onion, sliced *(optional)*

The first thing you're going to do is split the nostrils, making a cut all the way through, so that the snout lays out flat. Then you're going to flip it over to where you can see the fat and the tendons inside the snout; cut out the tendons you see—there's generally one on each side (those tendons work the hog's nose up and down, like when you see him moving his nose like a big-ass rabbit, and they help him snort). The next thing you're going to do is go in with a sharp knife and score the snout, making a cut about ⅜ inch (1 cm) deep, making cuts all the way across, then in the other direction to make a checkerboard. The scoring's going to help keep that snoot from curling up when you cook it: You want it to lay flat.

Flip the snout over and score it on the other side, taking care not to cut all the way through—you just want to score it. Now we take our mop and we're going to spritz it on both sides of the snout and season both sides with salt and pepper. Then we put the snout meat side down on the grate of our pit. We're going to shovel the coals underneath our pit, and we're going to cook the snout for 1½ to 2 hours so it gets good and crispy. Then we're going to come in and flip it upside down so it's skin side down now, and we're going to get it good and crispy on the bottom, so when you bite into the skin it'll be crunchy. That's going to take you about another 2 hours. The snout is already going to be about sandwich size, so lay it on some fresh bread, put a dab of barbecue sauce on the fat side, add maybe a dill pickle or two and some sliced onions on there, and you've got yourself a crunchy rooter sandwich.

PORK
CRACKLIN'S

The pork cracklings, or pork skins, are better than any damn skins you'll ever have because you can't buy these out of a bag—that crap you buy out of a bag is just puffed air and fat. This right here made with the skin of a hog is the real deal. We get the skin that cracklings are made from after we get through barbecuing our shoulders, our hams, and even our whole hog.

Makes:

4 TO 8 SERVINGS

ingredients

Vinegar-Based Barbecue Sauce *(page 55)*

Pork skin (1 pound / 0.5 kg pork skin yields about 8 cups / 1.2 g cracklin's, enough to serve 4 for snacks; 2 pounds / 0.9 kg pork fat yields enough to serve 8 for snacks)

What you have after you make a whole hog is skin that's crispy but not so much that you can bite through it. Once you get your meat ready to eat, you've got skin leftover. Bring the temperature to 265°F (130°C). Take that skin, lay it out flat, then take a thin-edged spoon and scrape all that fat out and render it down into lard (which you can save for Smoked Blackberry Cobbler, *page 214*). Apply a thin coating of salt and pepper onto that skin and put it into the pit, situating it on the grate with the scraped-out side down. And start shoveling them coals again. After an hour, you should see the edges starting to curl; flip the skin. Continue to cook the skin, back skin side down, for another hour. To check for doneness, bend the skin; it's ready when it begins to break. Then come in and lightly brush a little bit of your vinegar-based sauce onto the inside part of the skins, the side where you scraped the fat off. Cook for 5 or 10 minutes more, and you're good to go.

BRUNSWICK STEW

This is my family's version of the classic barbecue side dish, which was born in the town of Brunswick, Georgia (don't believe the folks who say it was born in Brunswick County, Virginia). This is an ideal dish for a crowd because it's hearty and delicious and simple; feel free to double the recipe and store a batch in the freezer or just have a giant shindig if you feel like it. It's best served with cornbread *(page 213)* alongside it.

Makes:

20 TO 25 SERVINGS

ingredients

4 pounds (1.8 kg) russet potatoes, peeled and quartered or coarsely chopped, depending on your preference

1½ pounds (0.7 kg) yellow onions, quartered

3 pounds (1.4 kg) smoked pulled pork *(page 82)*, finely shredded

½ cup (100 g) sugar

3 pounds (1.4 kg) canned crushed tomatoes

3 pounds (1.4 kg) canned creamed corn

3 pounds (1.4 kg) canned tomato sauce

2 cups (480 ml) Vinegar-Based Barbecue Sauce *(page 55)* or other favorite barbecue sauce

Preheat the oven to 300°F (150°C).

Combine all the ingredients and divide them evenly between two deep 13 x 9-inch (33 x 23-cm) roasting pans. Cover the pans with foil, put them in the oven, and bake, stirring frequently and making sure no meat sticks to the bottom of the pans, for 2½ to 3 hours, until the onions are tender. Serve warm in bowls.

HOG-SKIN
COLLARDS

This is a great side dish for any type of barbecue: classic collards. When I'm cooking hogs in my masonry pit I like to add hog skin to the collards to give them smoky flavor and also because that hog fat is going to make them shiny and bright to look at and extra tender to eat.

Makes:

10 TO 12 SERVINGS

ingredients

1 pound (0.5 kg) hog skin, taken from the shoulder or the ham of a fully smoked whole hog *(page 63)*

1 pound (0.5 kg) salt-cured pork, such as hog tails or jowls or thick-cut bacon, coarsely chopped

6 pounds (2.7 kg) collard greens, stems discarded, leaves cut into ½-inch to 1-inch (12-mm to 2.5-cm) strips

1 head young green cabbage, coarsely chopped

While the smoked whole hog is resting, find about a pound of skin from its shoulder or ham—there is a lot of extra skin on the hog, so this shouldn't be difficult. Cut the skin into 1-inch (2.5-cm) pieces.

In a large stockpot, cook the skin and the salt-cured pork together over moderately high heat, turning, until both are golden, about 4 minutes. Add about 7 quarts (6.6 L) water and bring to a boil. Simmer over low heat until the skin is tender, about 45 minutes. Bring the broth to a vigorous boil. Add large handfuls of the collards at a time, alternating with the cabbage, allowing each batch to wilt slightly before adding more. Return the broth to a boil. Reduce the heat and simmer the collards over medium heat, stirring occasionally, until they are tender, about 30 minutes. Taste the collards; they should be salty enough from the salt-cured meat, but if they're not, adjust for seasoning. Then transfer the collards to a large serving bowl, spoon some of the broth over the greens, and serve piping hot. Serve with Smoked Cornbread *(page 213)*.

CHAPTER 3:

BIRDS

WHOLE BIRDS

I felt like the whole world's love affair with chicken kind of passed us by down here in the Deep South—yes, we barbecued chicken for our church suppers and we sure fried it, but if there was pork, we ate pork. I didn't pay very much mind to how to cook chicken until I got serious about cooking barbecue professionally and I had to learn how to cook it better than everybody else so I could make some money. My dad loved to make half chickens *(page 127)*, so I'm going to give you his method for that—that's what he sold for take-out in his barbecue business and what I saw him cooking when I was coming up. The rest of these recipes for birds are ones that I figured out how to make on my own.

Right now everything that's popular revolves around

THE SOUTH.

A big part of that is barbecue. I learned from my dad,
who learned from his dad, who learned from his dad.

SMOKED
BUTTERFLIED
CHICKEN

The fastest and most efficient way to cook a chicken in a smoker is by spatchcocking it, which is a cool old-fashioned word for butterflying it. This lets you flatten the bird out for more even, consistent cooking of the breast and legs together, and shaves hours off your smoking time.

Cooking time:	Makes:
3 TO 4 HOURS	**2 TO 4 SERVINGS**

ingredients

1 (3½-pound / 1⅔-kg) whole chicken with the skin on

Distilled white vinegar

Kosher salt and freshly ground black pepper

Pit Mop *(page 57)*

Vinegar-Based Barbecue Sauce *(page 55)*

1: SELECT AND PREP THE MEAT

I like a whole chicken that's on the big side, so at least 3½ pounds (1⅔ kg). Local birds that didn't have to travel too far to get to your plate are best.

First, remove the neck and giblets. Rinse the chicken thoroughly in cold water and pat it dry with paper towels or a clean kitchen towel. To butterfly it: Place the chicken on a cutting board, breast side down. Using a very sharp kitchen knife or cleaver or sharp kitchen shears and working from the cavity opening to the neck, cut down the backbone of each side of the chicken; discard the backbone. Next, cut a 2-inch (5-cm) slit through the membrane and cartilage at the "V" of the neck end. Grab a breast in each hand and gently bend both sides backward, as if you were opening a book, to snap

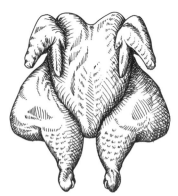

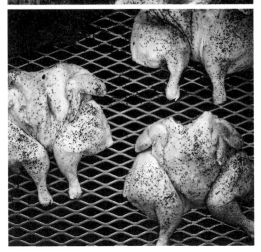

the breastbone. Use your fingers to work along both sides of the breastbone to loosen the triangular keel bone; pull out the bone. With the tip of a sharp knife, cut along both sides of the cartilage at the end of the breastbone; remove the cartilage. Now your chicken is good to go. Just rub it down inside and out with white vinegar, and then season it all over, the skin and the cavity, with salt and pepper.

2: PREPARE THE PIT OR SMOKER AND PUT THE MEAT ON *(see pages 41-51 for details)*

Place the bird in the pit, breast side up, and then start shoveling your coals underneath.

3: KEEP THE TEMP CONSISTENT, MOP THE BIRD

Every hour, mop the chicken thoroughly with the mop.

4: TEST FOR DONENESS

After 3 hours, check the Jack Mixon way: Pull on the leg and see if it easily twists away from the thigh; if it resists and doesn't turn, you're not done yet. Or use your instant-read thermometer: The breast should be 165°F (75°C), and the dark meat should reach 180°F (82°C).

5: PULL AND EAT THAT MEAT

Carefully and gently transfer the chicken from the pit to rest on its back on a cutting board or platter, uncovered, for 15 minutes. Then you can carve it and enjoy it.

IN THE SMOKER

Here's a down-and-dirty easy method to smoke a whole chicken in any type of smoker, including the one you may already have in your backyard:

PREP:

You do not need to butterfly the chicken to cook it in an offset smoker—it's less essential to prepare it that way because you can cook it for less time in the offset smoker than in the pit. You need a small whole chicken, about 3 pounds (1.4 kg). Apply white vinegar, salt, and pepper all over the chicken, inside and out, including on the skin, taking care to sprinkle the salt and pepper throughout the cavity. Let the chicken rest this way for 1 hour while you light the coals in the smoker and heat it to 250°F (120°C). Place the chicken on the smoker breast side up.

COOK:

Let the chicken smoke for about 3 hours, or until the internal temperature of the leg and thigh reaches 180°F (82°C). Remove the chicken from the smoker and allow it to rest for 15 minutes.

EAT:

To serve, carve the chicken into individual pieces, either 8 or 10 (2 wings, 2 breasts, 2 thighs, and 2 drumsticks; or divide the breast into two halves to make 10 pieces total).

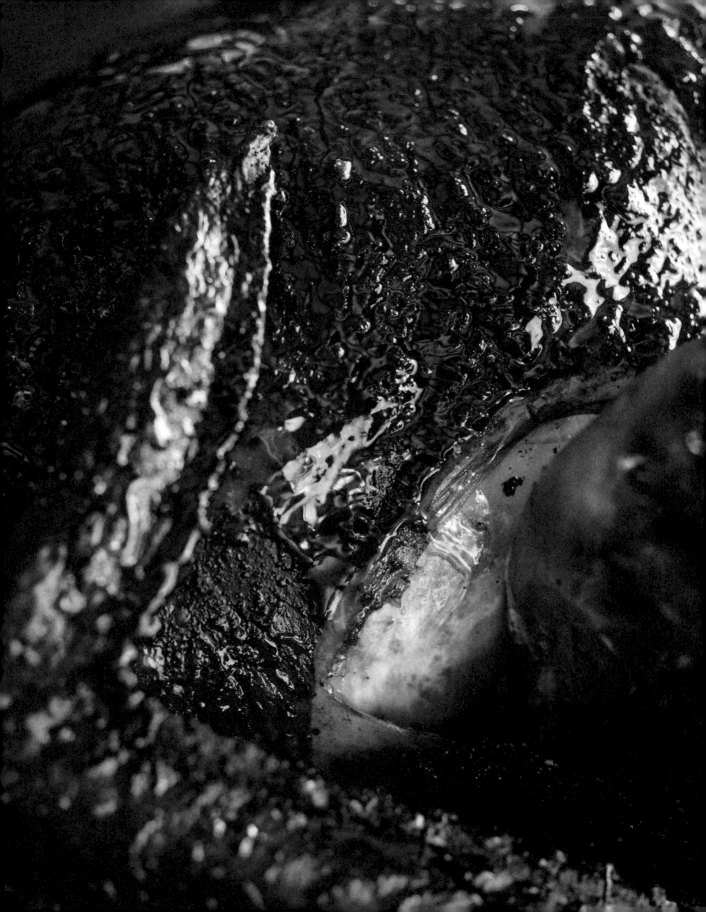

SMOKED
WHOLE TURKEY

Thanksgiving is the one holiday I don't cook. We go to the mountains on Thanksgiving. That said, I love smoked turkey and I don't believe you have to wait until Thanksgiving to enjoy it. I love a pulled turkey sandwich the next day, too.

Cooking time:

ABOUT 6 HOURS

Makes:

10 TO 12 SERVINGS

ingredients

1 (14- to 17-pound / 6.3- to 7.7-kg) turkey with skin on, neck and giblets removed

Pit Brine *(page 56)*

Distilled white vinegar

Kosher salt and freshly ground black pepper

Pit Mop *(page 57)*

Vinegar-Based Barbecue Sauce *(page 55)*

1: SELECT AND PREP THE MEAT

I like a turkey that is 14 to 17 pounds (6.3 to 7.7 kg). Remove the neck and giblets and use them to make your gravy, if you like.

One thing I do that my daddy didn't is brine the bird. The white meat really benefits from some additional flavor. Whip up a batch of Pit Brine, then submerge the turkey in the brine in a container large enough to hold it and let it sit overnight in the refrigerator. (You can also put it in an ice-packed cooler). When you're ready to cook it, bring the turkey out of the brine (discard the brine), then pat it dry thoroughly inside and out. Rub that turkey down inside and out with white vinegar. Then season it liberally with salt and pepper. Note that a turkey has got a lot of thick skin, and you need a heavy coating of salt and pepper on there.

2: PREPARE THE PIT OR SMOKER AND PUT THE MEAT ON *(see pages 41-51 for details)*

Bring the temperature to 265°F (130°C). We put the turkey on the grate in the pit breast side up.

3: KEEP THE TEMP CONSISTENT, MOP THE BIRD

We don't need to flip a whole turkey; not only is it too large, it's not flat, either, and you have to worry about keeping that meat moist inside the skin. So we're not going to touch it—we're going to let it sit and accumulate its juices without knocking it around too much. It takes longer to cook a turkey this way than if we butterfly it, but we keep our beautiful presentation intact. We are going to mop it every hour with our mop.

4: TEST FOR DONENESS

At the 5-hour mark, take a look at the turkey skin on the thigh. Take your finger and push down on the skin and see if the push leaves a dimple. If that happens, it's on the way to being done. If you want to use a meat thermometer, check that the thigh meat and leg

meat are around 180 to 185°F (82 to 85°C). You can also check by grabbing that drumstick and twisting it until it breaks away easily from that bird; when it does, you're ready to rock and roll. The breast meat's going to be somewhere around 165°F (75°C) when it's ready to pull off the pit.

5: PULL AND EAT THAT MEAT

Carefully and gently transfer the turkey from the pit to a wooden cutting board or platter. Allow the turkey to rest, loosely covered with foil, for 30 minutes. Then carve the turkey and serve immediately.

A NOTE ABOUT CARVING THE TURKEY

A lot of times you see people carving turkeys at Christmas and Thanksgiving, and they carve it all wrong: They go up in there and they just carve the breast lengthwise, which is the quickest way to dry out the meat on the bone. Instead, try it my way: Take your knife and go on and bone out that breast—remove the whole breast from the bird—then cut across it horizontally, using short strokes instead of long strokes, so you're cutting across the grain. Your turkey meat will be so much more moist, tender, and juicy this way. You can thank me later.

IN THE SMOKER

PREP:

I make a slightly smaller turkey in my smoker than in my pit, simply because I have less room. So here I'm talking about a 12- to 15-pound (5.4- to 6.8-kg) turkey, neck and giblets removed. You're going to brine that turkey with our Pit Brine *(page 56)* overnight. When you're ready to cook the turkey, discard the brine, pat it dry thoroughly, and place it in a large, deep aluminum pan to rest while you heat your smoker to 250°F (120°C).

COOK:

Transfer the turkey from the pan to the rack in the smoker breast side up and cook for 5 hours, or until the leg and thigh meat reaches an internal temperature of 180°F (82°C).

EAT:

Remove the turkey from the smoker and transfer it to a large, heavy cutting board or platter. Allow the turkey to rest, loosely covered with foil, for 30 minutes. Then carve the turkey and serve immediately.

Smoked Butterflied Turkey

If coming to the table with the big whole bird is not your priority, consider butterflying the turkey; it makes it quicker to cook and easier to handle since it's basically broken down into pieces. Butterflying your turkey is very similar to butterflying a whole chicken (see page 113): Set the turkey breast side down on a large cutting board with the tail closest to you. Use an electric knife or heavy-duty kitchen shears to cut up one side of the backbone. Turn the bird around and cut back down the other side of the spine. Reserve the backbone for Smoked Turkey Stock (page 148), if you like. Discard any fat pockets or excess skin found inside the turkey. Turn the turkey breast side up and use the heels of your hands to press down on both breasts until you hear a cracking sound and the bird has flattened slightly. Turn the turkey over onto what once was its back, splaying its legs out. Press hard on the ridge of the breastbone; you will hear a few cracks, and the turkey should now rest flatter—better for even cooking and crisper skin. Tuck the wing tips behind the breasts. Then proceed with the recipe as described on page 121: Use the Pit Brine (page 56) to brine the turkey overnight.

Bring the smoker temperature to 265°F (130°C). Then remove the turkey from the brine and discard the brine and pat the turkey dry with clean kitchen towels or paper towels. Spritz the turkey all over with white vinegar. Season the turkey all over with salt and pepper. Then put it on your smoker breast- side up, butterflied side down.

We're looking at a 4- to 5-hour cook time, mopping the bird with our Pit Mop (page 57) every hour. Start checking for doneness at the 5-hour mark. Do it the Jack Mixon way: Push down with your finger on the outside of the skin of the thigh; when you see that skin start to dimple, try to twist the leg away from the side of the breast meat where it connects; if it pulls easily, the turkey is ready to come off the pit. (You can use your instant-read thermometer, too: Look for the thighs and legs to hit 180°F / 82°C just as the breasts hit 165°F / 75°C.) Then you can rest and carve the turkey as described on page 117.

BIRD PARTS

If you've ever seen me on television talking about food that people like to eat, you've probably heard my theory about food with handles. It is my fervent belief that people like to eat food that's easy to pick up and hold—it solves a whole lot of problems when you're ready to chow down. Chicken "parts"—or cut-up pieces, if you will—have the kind of handles I'm always talking about; they make it easier for you to socialize while you're eating, and thus are great party foods. Speaking for myself, there's very little in life I like more than a chicken or turkey wing, let me tell you.

SMOKED
HALF CHICKENS

In my daddy's barbecue business, he preferred to cook chicken halves—and he cooked a whole lot of them. One of the main things you see when you're down in the South is half-chicken dinner fund-raisers. When you're raising money for the local Little League, you bet there's going to be half-chicken plates. We never cooked whole chickens, and we never cooked chicken pieces; although I cook both of those things now, for me the "original" way of making chicken is a half chicken. The chicken half is made up of a breast, a leg, a thigh, and a wing, and that will be enough meat right there to fill up anybody around.

Cooking time: | Makes:
3 TO 5 HOURS | **AT LEAST 2 SERVINGS**

ingredients

1 (3½-pound / 1.6-kg) whole chicken with the skin on, split in half

Distilled white vinegar

Kosher salt and freshly ground black pepper

Pit Mop (*page 57*)

Vinegar-Based Barbecue Sauce (*page 55*)

1: SELECT AND PREP THE MEAT

We buy whole chickens, local ones, and then we split them ourselves.

First, remove the neck and giblets. Place the chicken on a cutting board, breast side down. Using a very sharp kitchen knife or cleaver or sharp kitchen shears and working from the cavity opening to the neck, cut down the backbone of each side of the chicken; discard the backbone. Next, cut a 2-inch (5-cm) slit through the membrane and cartilage at the "V" of the neck end. Grab a breast in each hand and gently bend both sides backward, as if you were opening a book, to snap the breastbone. Use your fingers to work along both sides of the breastbone to loosen the triangular keel bone; pull out the bone. With the tip of a sharp knife, cut along both sides of the cartilage at the end of the breastbone; remove the cartilage. Turn the chicken breast side up. Cut lengthwise down the center of the chicken to split it into two halves.

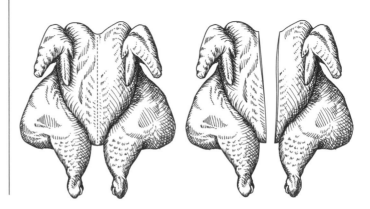

Rub each chicken half inside and out, skin and cavity, with white vinegar. Then season them thoroughly all over with salt and pepper—take your time to season the chicken.

2: PREPARE THE PIT OR SMOKER AND PUT THE MEAT ON *(see pages 41-51 for details)*

Bring the temperature to 265°F (130°C). Place the half chickens in the pit meat side down, bone side up.

3: KEEP THE TEMP CONSISTENT, MOP THE BIRD

Chickens do not have to be flipped, but they do have to be mopped. So while you're carefully keeping your pit temp consistent, you're going to mop them every hour all over—3 hours of cooking time means you'll mop three times.

4: TEST FOR DONENESS

At the 3-hour mark, take a look at the chicken skin. Take your finger and push down on the skin and see if the push leaves a dimple. If that happens, it's on the way to being done. The final check for doneness is to grab that chicken leg and gently twist it; if it pulls away easily, it is ready to go. The internal temperature should be 180°F (82°C).

5: PULL AND EAT THAT MEAT

Remove the chicken halves from the pit, carefully transfer them to a wooden cutting board or platter, and let them rest, uncovered, for 15 minutes. Then serve your birds—I give a half chicken per person.

IN THE SMOKER

You can make smoked half chickens in the offset smoker exactly in the way that you'd make a whole chicken (page 113). The cooking method is identical.

PREP:

You need a small whole chicken, about 3 pounds (1.4 kg) with the skin on, split in half. Apply white vinegar, salt, and pepper all over the chicken halves, inside and out, including on the skin, taking care to sprinkle the salt and pepper throughout the cavity. Let the chicken halves rest this way for 1 hour while you light the coals in the smoker and heat it to 250°F (120°C). Place the chicken halves on the smoker breast side up.

COOK:

Let the chicken smoke for about 3 hours, or until the internal temperature of the leg and thigh reaches 180°F (82°C). Remove the chicken from the smoker and allow it to rest on the rack in its pan for 15 minutes.

EAT:

Serve half a chicken to each person.

SMOKED
CHICKEN
WINGS

Breast man, leg man—whatever. I'm a wing man myself. By that I mean I could eat chicken wings all day. I just like the fact that you get a two-in-one eating experience: the drumette and the flat. Chicken wings are considered bar food, but I maintain that they're some of the best eating you can enjoy. Here I'm going to tell you how to make those wings get that one-of-a-kind pit-smoked flavor.

Cooking time:

2 HOURS

Makes:

12 WINGS

ingredients

12 chicken wings

Distilled white vinegar

Kosher salt and freshly ground black pepper

Pit Mop *(page 57)*

Vinegar-Based Barbecue Sauce *(page 55; optional)*

1: SELECT AND PREP THE MEAT

You need at least a dozen high-quality chicken wings, nice and meaty—the meatier they are, the better they'll do in the pit.

Rinse the wings thoroughly in cold water and pat them dry. Spritz thoroughly with white vinegar, then season them liberally all over on both sides with salt and pepper.

2: PREPARE THE PIT OR SMOKER AND PUT THE MEAT ON *(see pages 41-51 for details)*

Bring the temperature to 265°F (130°C). You're going to put the chicken wings on the grate over the coals in the smoker. Take care not to overlap them.

3: KEEP THE TEMP CONSISTENT, FLIP THE WINGS, MOP THE WINGS

These wings have a 2-hour cook time. Every 30 minutes, you're going to flip them, then mop them with the mop.

4: TEST FOR DONENESS

When the wings are close to the end of the 2-hour cook time, take the largest wing and pull the "drummie" from the flat. If it pulls easily, they're done. (Alternatively: When the drummies reach an internal temperature of 165°F / 75°C on a meat probe, they're done.)

5: PULL AND EAT THAT MEAT

Transfer the wings to a wooden cutting board or platter, cover them loosely with foil, and let them rest for 15 minutes. Serve them with some barbecue sauce on the side, if you like.

IN THE SMOKER

PREP:

Using a very sharp knife, cut each wing in half to separate the flat from the drumette. Rinse the pieces well and pat them dry. Spritz each all over with white vinegar. Liberally season each piece with salt and pepper. Place the chicken wings in an aluminum baking pan and let them rest while you heat your smoker to 250°F (120°C).

COOK:

Transfer the wings from the pan directly onto the grate in the smoker and cook the wings for 2 hours.

EAT:

Remove the wings from the smoker, brush them all over with Vinegar-Based Barbecue Sauce *(page 55)*, and return the pan to the smoker. Cook for 15 minutes. Transfer the wings to a cutting board, cover loosely with foil, and let rest for about 15 minutes. Uncover and enjoy with a little dipping sauce *(page 55)* on the side, if you like.

SMOKED
TURKEY
LEGS

We all love to eat turkey drumsticks because they've got a handle on them; you can hold them and gnaw down until your heart is content. This book ain't about a damn barbecue contest; if anything it's about a barbecue *eating* contest, and that's what turkey legs are good for: They're fun to eat.

Cooking time:	Makes:
ABOUT 4 HOURS	**4 SERVINGS**

ingredients

4 legs from 15- to 17-pound (6.8- to 7.7-kg) turkeys, skin on

Pit Brine *(page 56)*

Distilled white vinegar

Kosher salt and freshly ground black pepper

Pit Mop *(page 57)*

Vinegar-Based Barbecue Sauce *(page 55)*

1: SELECT AND PREP THE MEAT

The best turkey legs are coming off a large bird, a 15- to 17-pounder (6.8 to 7.7 kg). You'll likely have to get these from your butcher, but I see them sometimes in my supermarket, too.

These guys need to be brined overnight in our pit brine in the refrigerator. When you're ready to cook them, take them out of the brine, discard the brine, and pat the legs dry thoroughly with a clean kitchen towel or paper towels. Spritz them all over with white vinegar, then season them liberally on all sides with salt and pepper.

2: PREPARE THE PIT OR SMOKER AND PUT THE MEAT ON *(see pages 41-51 for details)*

Bring the temperature to 265°F (130°C). Then just put the legs in the pit.

3: KEEP THE TEMP CONSISTENT, FLIP THE LEGS, MOP THE LEGS

Every 30 minutes, turn the legs over and mop them with the mop.

4: TEST FOR DONENESS

At the 3½-hour mark, take a look at the turkey skin. Take your finger and push down on the skin and see if that push leaves a dimple. If that happens, it's on the way to being done. If you want to use a meat thermometer, check that the meat is around 180 to 185°F (82 to 85°C).

5: PULL AND EAT THAT MEAT

Pull the legs off the pit and transfer them to a wooden cutting board or platter. Let them rest, loosely covered with foil, for 15 minutes. Then chow down.

IN THE SMOKER

PREP:

The turkey legs need to be brined overnight in the Pit Brine *(page 56)* in the refrigerator. Remove the turkey legs from the brine and pat them dry thoroughly with paper towels. Spritz the legs all over with white vinegar, and then season them liberally all over with salt and pepper. Transfer them to a deep aluminum pan and let them rest while you heat your smoker to 250°F (120°C).

COOK:

Transfer the legs from the pan directly onto the grate of the smoker. Smoke the legs for 3 hours, or until the temperature of the legs in the meatiest part reaches 180°F (82°C) on an instant-read thermometer. Pull the legs from the smoker, wrap each individually in foil, and let them rest for 30 minutes.

EAT:

Remove the legs from the foil and serve with Vinegar-Based Barbecue Sauce *(page 55)* on the side for dipping.

Hawkinsville
Harvest Fest
Pigs & Produce BBQ
Jack's
OLD SOUTH

I was raised

SHOVELING COALS

under masonry pits. That was the only way barbecue was done.
That was the way our forefathers did it.

SMOKED
TURKEY
WINGS

Gobbler wings are the best damn wings on the planet, and I like ones that come from larger birds, 15 to 18 pounds (6.8 to 8.2 kg), and I don't take the tips off them because I'm going to gnaw down on those—I suggest you try them, too.

Cooking time:	Makes:
ABOUT 4 HOURS	**6 TO 8 SERVINGS**

ingredients

5 lbs (2.27 kg) turkey wings, skin on

Pit Brine *(page 56)*

Distilled white vinegar

Kosher salt and freshly ground black pepper

Pit Mop *(page 57)*, **some kept aside for serving, if desired**

Vinegar-Based Barbecue Sauce *(page 55; optional)*

1: SELECT AND PREP THE MEAT

We need to brine these turkey wings in our Pit Brine in the refrigerator overnight. When you're ready to cook them, remove them from the brine, discard the brine, and pat them dry thoroughly with a clean kitchen towel. Spritz them all over with white vinegar and season with salt and pepper.

2: PREPARE THE PIT OR SMOKER AND PUT THE MEAT ON *(see pages 41-51 for details)*

Bring the temperature to 265°F (130°C). I like to place these on the grate over the coals in the pit so that the wing tips are pointing away from the flame; otherwise they may burn at the tips.

3: KEEP THE TEMP CONSISTENT, MOP THE WINGS

We're going to mop the wings every hour with our mop. You don't usually have to flip these, but they do need checking: I always check them to see if the bottoms (tips) are getting too hot, and if they are, you should flip them.

4: TEST FOR DONENESS

At the 3½-hour mark, take a look at the turkey skin. Take your finger and push down on the skin and see if that push leaves a dimple. If that happens, they're on the way to being done. If you want to use a meat thermometer, check that the meat is around 180 to 185°F (82 to 85°C).

5: PULL AND EAT THAT MEAT

Bring the wings out of the pit and transfer them to a wooden cutting board or platter and let them rest, loosely covered with foil, for 15 minutes. You can serve these with some fresh mop or some barbecue sauce on the side for dipping, if you like. Add this at the end: When the wings are cool enough to handle, use a sharp knife to cut the wings into three sections—drumette, wingette, and tip. Serve with Vinegar-Based Barbecue Sauce (page 55).

IN THE SMOKER

PREP:

Brine the wings overnight in the Pit Brine *(page 56)* in the refrigerator. When ready to cook, pull them from the brine, discard the brine, and pat them dry thoroughly with paper towels. Spritz the wings all over with vinegar and season them liberally with salt and pepper on all sides. Place them in a deep aluminum pan and let them rest while you heat your smoker to 250°F (120°C).

COOK:

Transfer the wings from the pan to the grate of the smoker. Smoke the wings for 3 hours, or until the temperature in the meatiest part reaches 180°F (82°C) on an instant-read thermometer. Pull the wings and let them rest on a cutting board or platter, loosely covered with foil, for 30 minutes.

EAT:

Uncover the wings and serve with Vinegar-Based Barbecue Sauce *(page 55)* on the side for dipping.

BIRD EXTRAS

I may not have always understood America's love affair with chicken, but no one had to tell me twice when it comes to what's great about sandwiches. My sandwiches are not complicated, big, stacked-up layered things that cost you $14 apiece; they are simple homemade sandwiches that are all about that flavor that the pit gives the bird. The turkey sandwich is a sneaky treat I give myself, a reward for making the turkey for everybody else to enjoy; the chicken salad is my light weekday work lunch (enhanced with Georgia pecans, of course), and the stock is something useful for all cooks to have around—and this version made from smoky bones is a damn sight better than anything you can get in a can at the supermarket.

THE
PITMASTER'S
TURKEY SANDWICH

Some of the best barbecue you'll ever have is during your private pitmaster time: When you're cooking a turkey on the pit, before you serve it you pull some meat off for yourself, right then and there on the spot, and make yourself a little secret treat. Just pile up the turkey meat (make sure you get some of that crispy skin on it) and some dill pickles—I love dill pickles with my barbecue—on white bread. I think white bread is underrated—and I also think it's the best stuff for this sandwich.

Makes:

1 BIG BAD SANDWICH

ingredients

2 slices white bread, home-made or store-bought

2 tablespoons mayonnaise, homemade or your favorite brand

Kosher salt and freshly ground black pepper

1 cup (195 g) freshly pulled smoked turkey meat *(page 117)* **from the underside of the turkey (so folks can still see the bird looking pretty when you serve it)**

Dill pickles, sliced

Lay out the slices of bread and spread mayonnaise on one side of each slice. Season liberally with salt and pepper. On one piece of bread, pile on your turkey meat, taking care to evenly distribute it all over the slice. Lay pickle slices on top of the turkey meat. Close the sandwich with the other prepared piece of bread. And don't tell anyone you did it—it's that good.

SMOKED
CHICKEN or TURKEY
PITMASTER STOCK

This recipe is going to be the same whether you're using chicken or turkey. You're going to save the bones of the smoked meat and turn them into this delicious stock. Because the birds have been smoked, your stock will have a distinct rich flavor; you can make chicken noodle soup out of it or use it for sauces and gravies just like you would any other kind of stock. But it will be better, because this is Pitmaster Stock.

Makes:

ABOUT 3 QUARTS (2.8 L)

ingredients

1 large smoked chicken or turkey carcass, legs, or wings *(pages 113–42)*, chopped into manageable pieces to fit into a pot

8 cloves garlic, unpeeled and smashed

2 stalks celery, coarsely chopped

1 medium onion, quartered

2 large carrots, peeled and coarsely chopped

1 bay leaf

Kosher salt and freshly ground black pepper

In a large heavy Dutch oven or stockpot, combine all the ingredients. Add enough cold water to submerge all the ingredients, about 3 quarts (2.8 L). Bring to a boil over high heat, use a slotted spoon to skim any scum from the surface, then turn the heat down to low to simmer. Simmer the stock gently for 3 to 4 hours, using a slotted spoon to skim occasionally. Remove from the heat and let the stock cool for about 30 minutes. Strain the stock through a fine sieve. Let cool completely, about another 30 minutes, then refrigerate. Once the stock is cold it should be amber in color and relatively clear. Divide it among plastic containers, leaving some space at the top for expansion if you plan to freeze it. The stock will keep in the refrigerator for about 5 days and in the freezer for about 3 months.

THE PITMASTER'S SMOKED
CHICKEN SALAD
SANDWICHES

I'm always thinking ahead when I'm cooking in my pit about what I'm going to eat for the week, and I'll throw on an extra half chicken *(page 127)* just so I can have chicken salad sandwiches. This is not a so-called tea sandwich: I like a chicken salad sandwich to be filling and full of different flavors and textures. I also like to mix in both white and dark meat; I don't get it when people ask me if I prefer white or dark meat—there's nothing wrong with either, in my book. And remember: I was raised on white bread (or "light bread," as we call it in the South), so that's what I like for this sandwich, but you should have it on any bread you like, or simply pile it up in a bowl and get yourself some saltines— that's a pitmaster's lunch for you right there.

Makes:

4 SANDWICHES

ingredients

About 4 cups (780 g) leftover pulled smoked chicken *(pages 113–5)*, white and dark meat

1 cup (240 ml) mayonnaise, homemade or your favorite brand

1 cup (180 g) chopped Granny Smith or other tart apple

½ cup (60 g) chopped pecans

4 hard-boiled eggs, chopped

1 cup (150 g) halved seedless red grapes

Kosher salt and freshly ground black pepper

8 slices white bread

Garnishes (optional): iceberg lettuce, tomato slices, and red onion slices

In a large bowl, combine the chicken, mayonnaise, apple, pecans, hard-boiled eggs, and grapes. Season generously with salt and pepper. Using a wooden spoon, gently mix the chicken salad together, taking care to thoroughly combine all the ingredients.

In the center of each of 4 slices of bread, scoop about one-quarter of the chicken salad and then use a spoon to spread it around gently to cover the whole slice of bread. Top with whichever garnishes you like—all of them or none of them—and place the other slice of bread on top of the sandwich.

RUMP
SIRLOIN
T-BONE
TENDERLOIN
RIB EYE
RIB
PRIME RIB
BLADE ROAST
CHUCK
SHOULDER
TONGUE
TOP SIRLOIN
SHORT LOIN
BOTTOM SIRLOIN
ROUND
BOTTOM ROUND
FLANK
PLATE
BRISKET
SHANK
SHANK

CHAPTER 4:
the
COW

BEEF CUTS

It's hard for me to think of these beef recipes without remembering all the competitions that it took for me to learn how to make them right—competition barbecue prizes sweetness, which requires complicated methods of injections, sauces, and rubs to achieve. Pit smoking for me marks a return to the special quality of beef's natural flavor, as it's enhanced only by the process of barbecuing. I think of beef as a luxury; we had it once a week when I was growing up and everybody looked forward to it. It still means a special occasion to me to this day; in fact, if I'm eating beef, I'm probably celebrating something or giving myself a hard-earned treat. The luxuriousness of velvety beef is not compromised in the pit, but rather enhanced—the combination of rich flavor kissed with the deep smoky essence of the pit is among the most mouthwatering sensations for pitmasters like me.

SMOKED
BEEF RIBS

Most folks don't realize that when it comes to the cow there are a few different things a person could mean when you say "ribs." You could mean the short ribs *(see page 151)* or you could mean the back ribs, the big guys, and that's what most barbecue guys are interested in because they're fun to cook—I call them "tenderlicious" because of how succulent they are when you cook them right.

Cooking time:	*Makes:*
ABOUT 4 HOURS AND 15 MINUTES	**4 SERVINGS**

ingredients

8 beef ribs

Distilled white vinegar

Kosher salt and freshly ground black pepper

Pit Mop *(page 57)*

Vinegar-Based Barbecue Sauce *(page 55)*

1: SELECT AND PREP THE MEAT

You can usually find beef ribs in most grocery meat departments sold in mini slabs of 3 or 4. If you want to make sure you're getting the best-quality beef available, I'd recommend getting them from a butcher. To feed 4 people, you need 8 whole beef ribs. Serving more people? Count on 2 for most folks, maybe 3 for your biggest eaters. (I often don't even eat 3 of these suckers, so keep that in mind.)

I suggest a small amount of trimming here: Peel off the thick membrane (or "silver skin," as it's called in the barbecue world) that covers the back side of each rib: It's easy to do if you work your fingers underneath the membrane until you have 2 to 3 inches (5 to 7.5 cm) cleared, then grab the membrane with a kitchen towel and pull it away from the rib and discard it. This will expose some loose fat if the rib has any, so if you see any excess fat, just use a paring knife and cut it out. Now spritz the ribs all over with white vinegar and season them all over, liberally, with salt and pepper.

2: PREPARE THE PIT OR SMOKER AND PUT THE MEAT ON *(see pages 41-51 for details)*

Bring the temperature to 265°F (130°C). Set the ribs on the grate in the pit meat side down, bone side up.

3: KEEP THE TEMP CONSISTENT, FLIP THE RIBS, MOP THE RIBS

We'll cook these ribs on the pit for 2 hours, then flip them over, mop them with the mop, and cook for 2 more hours, mopping every 20 minutes. After 4 hours pull the rib gently and feel for the bone to begin to slip from the meat. Then you can be sure you're done.

4: PULL AND EAT THAT MEAT

Use long, heavy-duty tongs to remove the ribs from the smoker. Transfer them to a platter or cutting board and let them rest, loosely covered, for 10 minutes. Then they're good to go. Serve alongside plenty of sauce for dipping

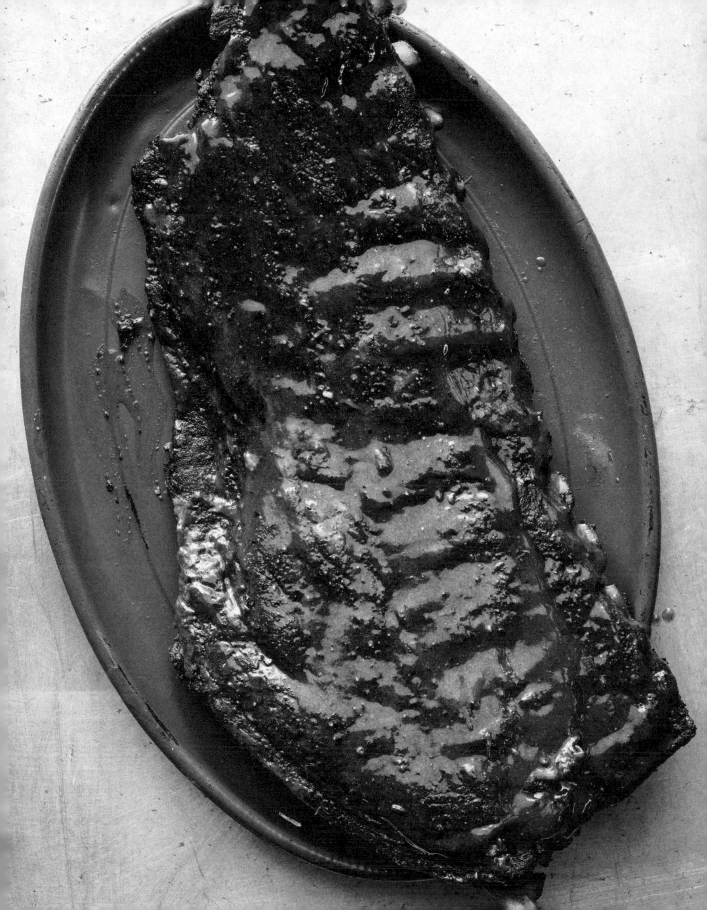

IN THE SMOKER

PREP:

Peel off the thick membrane (or "silver," as it's called in the barbecue world) that covers the back side of each rib: It's easy to do if you work your fingers underneath the membrane until you have 2 to 3 inches (5 to 7.5 cm) cleared, then grab the membrane with a kitchen towel and pull it away from the rib and discard it. This will expose some loose fat if the rib has any, so if you see any excess fat, just use a paring knife and cut it out. Now spritz the ribs all over with white vinegar and season them all over, liberally, with salt and pepper. Put the ribs in a deep aluminum pan and let them rest while you heat your smoker to 250°F (120°C).

COOK:

Transfer the ribs from the pan onto the grate of the smoker and cook for 2 hours. Remove the ribs from the smoker and transfer them to a large clean aluminum pan, meat side up. Pour 2 cups (480 ml) water into the pan, cover the pan with aluminum foil, and return it to the smoker for 2 more hours. At the 4-hour mark, remove the pan from the smoker and glaze the top of the ribs (only the top) with the Vinegar-Based Barbecue Sauce *(page 55)*—use just enough to coat the ribs, taking care not to over-sauce. Put the pan back in the smoker, uncovered, and cook for 15 minutes.

EAT:

Remove the pan from the smoker and let the ribs rest, loosely covered, for 10 minutes. Serve with more sauce on the side, if you like.

The EARLY DAYS *of* COMPETITION BARBECUE

I STARTED COMPETING in barbecue contests in June 1996. My dad, Jack, had died unexpectedly from a stroke six months before, when he was only fifty-six years old. I was thirty-two, I was divorced, I had to pay child support, I had to pay the bills, and I had two boys to feed. I got into competition barbecue because my mother's family made a good barbecue sauce that my parents were selling, and I wanted to promote it by going out and trying to win some trophies and gather some notoriety. Well, I did much more than that. The first contest I went to was the Lock-&-Dam BBQ Contest in Augusta, Georgia. I went by myself with no crew, and I took a first place in the whole-hog category. I said to myself, "This right here, I can do this."

At the time Pat Burke, a legendary pitmaster from Murphysboro, Illinois, was the man to beat. After my dad, Pat is my barbecue hero; he's eighty years old now, and we're still friends. When I was first getting into barbecue and doing local contests in Georgia, I knew I was never going to get any better if I kept going up against people who I knew I could beat. Pat was winning all the contests then, and I think even early on he respected and liked me, while he wanted to beat the breaks off everyone else out there. I was probably one of the first people who made a job out of competing on the barbecue contest circuit—I didn't have another job on the side like most folks did then and some still do now, and that gave me an edge. Most people were doing barbecue contests as a hobby and they didn't depend on competition money to pay their bills, but I figured out I could do it for a living because I got good at it.

Jack taught me the hardest way to cook pit barbecue there is, so when I started competing it was a piece of cake compared to what I had been doing for my dad. I understood the flavors of the meat and what complemented it, and I made a science of the barbecue cooking contests because I wanted to get better at it. At the early contests the people competing weren't necessarily the people who had a background in barbecue; contests were more like social gatherings, like competitions for something folks were doing in their backyards. Today barbecue has been brought to the forefront by television shows and people writing cookbooks, and the game is a whole lot more competitive. People are buying expensive equipment and going to cooking schools to speed up their learning curves. My education came from the Jack Mixon School of Barbecue. It's hard for me to win contests these days because I'm the Big Guy now. I'm on TV, I've won more contests than anyone else, and there's a target on my back. Others like me bring a notoriety to barbecue that wouldn't have happened if we weren't out there, but like any "hot" profession, there's always a desire for new faces and for a future generation of pitmasters to come along. Competitions want me to be there right now, but they don't want me to win.

SMOKED
BEEF SHORT RIBS

Hey, as long as you've got your pit up and smoking, you can throw some short ribs or ox-tails on there, too, but I don't usually cook these in my other smokers because they're small and somewhat unusual cuts.

Short ribs are the first through the fifth ribs that sit right under the neck of the animal and are usually 3 to 4 inches (7.5 to 10 cm) long. There's a nice long rectangle of well-marbled meat that sits on top of these short, wide bones; the fat in the marbling melts as these ribs cook, which keeps them moist, tender, and juicy. I like to eat these by dipping them in either some extra vinegar mop *(page 57)* or some good barbecue sauce *(page 55)*. The advantage they have is that compared to other beef ribs and pork ribs, they cook up relatively fast in the smoker.

Cooking time:	Makes:
2½ TO 3 HOURS	**4 TO 6 SERVINGS**

ingredients

3 to 4 pounds (1.4 to 1.8 kg) bone-in beef short ribs, each 2 to 4 inches (5 to 10 cm) long (6 to 8 pieces)

Distilled white vinegar

Kosher salt and freshly ground black pepper

Pit Mop *(page 57)*

Vinegar-Based Barbecue Sauce *(page 55)*

1: SELECT AND PREP THE MEAT
I often see short ribs in grocery store butcher counters, but if you want to make sure you're getting the best-quality beef available in your area, I'd recommend getting them from a butcher.

2: PREPARE THE PIT OR SMOKER AND PUT THE MEAT ON *(see pages 41-51 for details)*
Spritz the ribs all over on both sides with white vinegar. Then season them liberally all over with salt and pepper.

3: KEEP THE TEMP CONSISTENT, MOP THE RIBS
We need a steady 250°F (120°C) in the pit for these ribs. After the first hour, we're going to flip them and mop them with our mop, and repeat that process every 20 minutes for about 2 hours.

4: TEST FOR DONENESS
Start checking for doneness at the 2-hour mark. The short ribs are done when they are very dark brown and tender enough to pull apart. You will see that the meat has shrunk back from the ends of the bones by ¼ inch (6 mm) or so.

5: PULL AND EAT THAT MEAT
Transfer the short ribs to a wooden cutting board, cover with foil, and let rest for at least 5 minutes. Serve with barbecue sauce on the side.

SMOKED
BEEF TENDERLOIN

Beef tenderloin is pretty much synonymous with Christmas for some folks, or with an anniversary party or some other occasion when you're willing to splurge on a fancy, delicate cut of meat. I think if you're celebrating, beef tenderloin is worth it: The cut happens to contain a whole lot of natural flavor already, and it's meltingly tender to start with, so the only two ways you can screw it up are by overseasoning it or, worse, overcooking it. This meat should be cooked and enjoyed at medium-rare doneness and no more, so keep that in mind when you cook it—this is not the time to fall asleep at the pit.

Cooking time:	*Makes:*
ABOUT 1½ HOURS	**6 SERVINGS**

ingredients

1 (3-pound / 1.4-kg) beef tenderloin roast

Distilled white vinegar

Kosher salt and freshly ground black pepper

Pit Mop *(page 57)*

1: SELECT AND PREP THE MEAT

If you're going all out, go all out and get the best one you can. Overhandling tenderloin is the surest way to ruin it, so treat it with special care. With a cut this tender, there's not going to be anything to trim. Wipe the tenderloin down and pat it dry. Wipe it all over with white vinegar and season with salt and pepper.

2: PREPARE THE PIT OR SMOKER AND PUT THE MEAT ON *(see pages 41-51 for details)*

Transfer the tenderloin to a large heavy wide-bottomed aluminum pan. Bring the smoker temperature to 265°F (130°C), then put the pan in the smoker.

3: KEEP THE TEMP CONSISTENT, MOP THE TENDERLOIN

Cook for about 30 minutes, then go in and mop the tenderloin. At the 1-hour mark, hit it again all over with the mop and put the pan back in the smoker. Cook for 15 minutes more and use your instant-read thermometer to begin testing for doneness. It may take another 15 minutes.

4: TEST FOR DONENESS

Because we're taking care not to overcook this sucker, we're going to use a instant-read thermometer and remove it the minute we get to 125°F (52°C) for rare, 130 to 135°F (54 to 57°C) for medium rare—at that point we know we're done.

5: PULL AND EAT THAT MEAT

Transfer the tenderloin to a wooden cutting board and let it rest for 10 minutes. Cut the tenderloin crosswise against the grain into ½-inch-thick (12-mm-thick) slices and serve immediately.

IN THE SMOKER

PREP:

Use a clean kitchen towel or paper towels to pat the tenderloin dry. Spritz it all over with vinegar, then season it liberally on all sides with salt and pepper. Let the tenderloin rest in an aluminum roasting pan while you heat your smoker to 275°F (135°C).

COOK:

Transfer the tenderloin from the pan onto the grate in the smoker and cook for about 1½ hours, until the internal temperature at the center for the tenderloin reaches 125°F (52°C) for rare, 130 to 135°F (54 to 57°C) for medium rare. Transfer the tenderloin to a cutting board and let it rest for 10 minutes.

EAT:

Cut the tenderloin crosswise against the grain into ½-inch-thick (12-mm-thick) slices and serve immediately.

SMOKED
BRISKET

Let me tell you something humorous: I have so many prizes for cooking brisket, but I learned to cook a brisket backward: My dad never cooked it in his life. When we were growing up, I didn't know what a damn beef brisket was—we didn't eat or cook brisket, you didn't find them in the Deep South in supermarkets very often, and if we ever ate brisket it was ground up into hamburger meat at a restaurant. I taught myself how to cook brisket when I started competing seriously on the barbecue circuit by studying the meat and paying close attention to how other people I respected were handling it. Here's how I learned how to do it on masonry pits, which is by far the easiest way: We don't need brining, we don't need injecting—we keep it easy, and it's delicious.

Cooking time:

ABOUT 8 HOURS

Makes:

20 TO 25 SERVINGS

ingredients

1 (12- to 15-pound / 5.4- to 6.8-kg) untrimmed beef brisket

Distilled white vinegar

Kosher salt and freshly ground black pepper

Pit Mop (*page 57*)

1: SELECT AND PREP THE MEAT

I like a big beef brisket that hasn't been cut up or trimmed—a 12- to 15-pounder (5.4 to 6.8 kg) if you can find one. This just means I can feed a lot of people or have some excellent leftovers. Butcher shops and groceries usually cut briskets up into two pieces: the first or "flat" cut from the cow's belly and the second or "point" cut, which is near the foreshank. Both have pros and cons: The first cut is evenly shaped and lean; the second cut is fattier and tougher but has more flavor. I am giving you a recipe for a whole untrimmed brisket, which includes both the flat and the point; you may have to order directly from a butcher, but trust me, it's worth it: This is what I cook in my pits at home. And after buying meat from mass-market retailers and special-ordering it from top-notch purveyors, I have done enough homework that I can tell you that to make a great brisket, you have to start with great-quality meat. I like brisket from the Wagyu cattle, a breed first cultivated in Japan and prized for its fine marbling and rich flavor that you can now get in the United States. Get it if you can.

Before you can smoke your brisket you need to trim the membrane, which is the fine silvery-white weblike coating on the meat. Use a sharp paring knife and slowly separate and cut away the layers of sticky white matter that surround the meat. It may take a while, but if you don't do it—and keep in mind that I'm not the kind of guy who works hard when he doesn't have to—your meat will be tough,

so do a good solid job and take your time. When you're finished, use a kitchen towel or paper towel to rub the meat all over with white vinegar. Then season it liberally all over with salt and pepper.

2: PREPARE THE PIT OR SMOKER AND PUT THE MEAT ON *(see pages 41-51 for details)*

Once our pit is stable at 275°F (135°C), gently place the brisket, meat side down, fat side up, on the grate in the pit.

3: KEEP THE TEMP CONSISTENT, FLIP THE BRISKET, MOP THE BRISKET

Smoke the brisket for 3 hours to get a good crust on it. Then flip the brisket, which means the fat side will now be down and the meat side up. Mop the brisket all over with the mop. We're going to smoke the brisket like this for 5 more hours, mopping every 30 minutes.

4: TEST FOR DONENESS

Use an instant-read thermometer inserted in the point end to check the temperature: We're looking for 205°F (95°C). It may take as little as a few more minutes to get there or up to an hour more, so be sure to check it every 15 minutes after the 5-hour mark.

---

* Note: Guess what, folks? Because my dad never cooked a brisket, I don't have any tricks to check for doneness; even I use a meat thermometer on this one!

5: PULL AND EAT THAT MEAT

We pull the brisket off the smoker when the point end registers 205°F (95°C), and then we wrap it in foil and let it rest for 2 hours on a wooden cutting board. Then we slice the brisket against the grain, drizzle a little sauce on it if we feel like it, and enjoy something that's out of this world—it's so good I sometimes wish I could haul around a masonry pit to my competitions because I'd win every damn time.

IN THE SMOKER

PREP:

Trim the brisket: Using a sharp paring knife, slowly separate and cut away the layers of sticky white matter that surround the meat; take your time. When you're finished, use a kitchen towel or paper towel to rub the meat all over with white vinegar. This adds a layer of flavor, moistens the meat, and kills bacteria in the process. Then season it liberally all over with salt and pepper. Place the brisket in a deep aluminum baking pan and let it rest while you heat your smoker to 350°F (175°C).

COOK:

Transfer the brisket from the pan to the grate of the smoker and cook the brisket for 2½ hours. Remove the brisket from the smoker, cover it with foil, and place in a deep aluminum baking pan. Put the pan in the smoker and cook for another 1½ hours, or until the temperature in the point end of the meat reaches 205°F (95°C) on an instant-read thermometer. Remove the brisket from the smoker and pan and wrap the brisket, still covered with foil, in a thick blanket. (The blanket is my own personal technique that I discovered on the professional barbecue circuit for making sure that brisket gets nice and tender without drying out, and I use it in competition to this day.) Let it rest this way at room temperature for at least 2 hours.

EAT:

Remove the blanket, discard the foil, and set the brisket aside on a cutting board, taking care to save the accumulated juices. Pour off the clear fat that rests on top of the pan, taking care to retain the juices, then pour the juices into a medium saucepan. Warm the juices over medium heat and allow them to come to a simmer. Meanwhile, slice the brisket against the grain; try to make the slices as consistently sized as possible. Place the slices on a warmed platter and pour the juices over them. Serve immediately.

SMOKED
BEEF OXTAILS

If you're uninitiated, oxtail is just what it sounds like: the tail of the cattle. Butchers usually cut it into segments. Oxtails are enjoyed a lot in Europe, where it's something like a delicacy, and in the rural South, where we pride ourselves on eating all parts of an animal; mostly it's braised in soups and stews, but when you smoke it in the pit it takes on a delicious, gamy flavor.

Cooking time:

ABOUT 5 HOURS

Makes:

6 TO 8 SERVINGS

ingredients

6 pounds (2.7 kg) oxtails, cut into 2- to 3-inch (5- to 7.5-cm) pieces

Distilled white vinegar

Kosher salt and freshly ground black pepper

Pit Mop *(page 57)*

Vinegar-Based Barbecue Sauce *(page 55)*

1: SELECT AND PREP THE MEAT

You can get oxtails from any butcher, even the ones in the grocery store, but you will most likely have to ask.

Spritz your oxtails all over with white vinegar. Season them liberally all over with salt and pepper. Do any additional trimming to make sure the oxtail pieces are all about the same size and thus will cook evenly.

2: PREPARE THE PIT OR SMOKER AND PUT THE MEAT ON *(see pages 41-51 for details)*

Bring the temperature to 265°F (130°C). Put the oxtails on the grate in the pit, cut side down.

3: KEEP THE TEMP CONSISTENT, FLIP THE OX-TAILS, MOP THE OXTAILS

Smoke them for 3 hours. After 3 hours, flip them over to the other side and smoke them for 1½ hours. Transfer your oxtails to an aluminum baking pan. Pour in your mop until it reaches a little way up the side of the pan, about 1½ cups (360 ml) or so, depending on the size of your pan. Put the pan in the pit and smoke for another 1½ hours.

4: TEST FOR DONENESS

The oxtails should be crisp on the outside and tender when you push down on them with your index finger (if they're hard, they need a little more time).

5: PULL AND EAT THAT MEAT

Transfer the oxtails to a wooden cutting board, cover them loosely with foil, and let them rest for about 10 minutes before you gnaw down on them. There's not a ton of meat on oxtails, but they're fun to eat. Some chefs pull the meat off the bones and separate out the cartilage and use the oxtails in tacos or fold the meat into a rich gravy that you can serve atop grits, but I like eating them fresh out of the pit and straight off the bone myself.

SMOKED
PRIME RIB

I think that the best way to cook rib-eye steaks on our masonry pits is to prepare the whole rib-eye loin, or the prime rib. This meat has just about the most marbling you're going to get on a cow: This marbling means it has good fat content that makes for a good crust on the outside of the meat. Prime rib is an expensive, luxurious cut, so when you splurge on it and cook it, make it your showpiece for special occasions and holidays. Although your guests will think you worked very hard on it because of its fancy reputation, prime rib is very easy to do on a pit. With this cut, you don't need to do any injections or marinating—you need no damn pretending when you're cooking the real deal.

Cooking time:

ABOUT 3 HOURS

Makes:

10 TO 12 SERVINGS

ingredients

1 (5-rib) prime rib (10 to 12 pounds / 4.5 to 5.4 kg)

Distilled white vinegar

Kosher salt and freshly ground black pepper

Pit Mop (*page 57*)

Vinegar-Based Barbecue Sauce (*page 55*)

1: SELECT AND PREP THE MEAT

If you're going to invest in an expensive cut like prime rib, I suggest getting it from a butcher if you can. The most important thing to know is that there are actually two separate cuts that may be called "prime rib," so you need to make sure you're getting the right one. The first cut (ribs 1 through 3) is closer to the loin, so it's the most tender. The second cut (ribs 4 through 7) is closer to the chuck end and is denser and more fatty. Ask the butcher for the first cut, and buy the best quality you can afford. Note that I'm giving you a recipe here for what I consider a small roast—sometimes I cook a prime rib that's 20 pounds (9 kg) to feed my folk—so if you want to go big and scale this recipe up, that's easy to do if you know the rule of thumb: Allow 30 minutes per pound, which can be applied to a prime rib of any size.

All we need to do to prep the meat is use a sharp knife to trim any excess fat, but don't go crazy, because we want enough fat on the outside to give us that bubbling crust—so leave a good ½-inch (12-mm) border around the meat if you need to do any trimming. Then spritz the meat down with white vinegar, which gives it a base layer of flavor, makes it a little wet, and kills bacteria in the process. Now come in with salt and pepper and season the meat liberally all over.

2: PREPARE THE PIT OR SMOKER AND PUT THE MEAT ON *(see pages 41-51 for details)*

Bring the temperature to 265°F (130°C). Put the prime rib on the grate in the pit with the fat side down and the rib side up.

3: KEEP THE TEMP CONSISTENT, FLIP THE ROAST, MOP THE ROAST

Smoke it for 2 hours. At the 2-hour mark, we're going to go into our pit and flip the roast because we want to get a good crust all over it. At that point when we go in to flip, we're going to use our mop and mop the roast. We're going to continue mopping the roast every 30 minutes, taking care to hit the roast all over in order to impart that vinegar tang flavor in there with that beef.

4: TEST FOR DONENESS

At the 2½-hour mark, we're going to start testing for doneness. We're going to take the internal temperature right in the center of the roast and look for 165°F (75°C). The edges are going to be for someone like my dad who wants it dead and burnt, and at the center it's going to be more like a medium rare—good to eat.

5: PULL AND EAT THAT MEAT

You ain't gonna need a sauce for this; you ain't gonna need anything else, it's so delicious.

IN THE SMOKER

PREP:

All we need to do here is use a sharp knife to trim any excess fat, taking care to leave a good ½-inch (12-mm) layer over the meat to provide some flavor. Then spritz the meat down with white vinegar and come in with salt and pepper and season the meat thoroughly all over. Place the meat in a large aluminum roasting pan and let it rest while you heat the smoker to 250°F (120°C).

COOK:

Transfer the meat from the pan onto the grate of the smoker. Cook for 5 hours, or until the internal temperature reaches 130°F (55°C) on an instant-read thermometer when measured at the center of the roast, for medium rare. Transfer the meat to a platter or cutting board, cover it loosely with foil, and let it rest at room temperature for at least 1 hour.

EAT:

Unwrap the roast, reserving any accumulated juices. In a medium saucepan over medium heat, allow the drippings to simmer for a couple of minutes. Pour the heated drippings over the roast. Carve the roast and serve it immediately.

WHEN *the* WINNING IS DONE

BEING AT THE JACK DANIEL'S World Championship Invitational Barbecue Competition is a big deal; you've got the best teams from around the world there, including teams from Europe and Asia. There's one big party in Lynchburg, Tennessee, let me tell you. One year we had done really well in the competition and when the awards ceremony was over, we were partying down by the side of a creek on the competition site. We don't party when we're competing. But we had some celebrating to do. The creek water has a lot of iron it, which is why they like to make whiskey with it; at that time of year there was only about three feet of water in the creek. Canada sent a lot of teams that year, and I was drinking my Crown Royal and cheering for them.

Like everyone who drinks a lot of any liquid, I had to break water, as they say. There was a Porta-Potty about ten feet from where I was standing, but instead of going over to use it I decided I would just let go into the creek. So I'm standing on the edge of the creek and I got to wobbling . . . and before I knew it, I had rolled down the embankment about ten feet, right into the water. Everybody was looking down at me, and I'm on my side looking up, trying to figure out what in the hell happened. I tried to get out, but I knew I looked like one of them damn alligators trying to claw his way up a mud hill. On the bank folks were as drunk as I was, but one of them realized that there was a utility light pole near where I was, so he got the group to do a drunk human chain to try to reach me and get me out of that creek. Well, they about fell in trying.

Finally, three sober people came around and dragged me out of there. By that point I had algae and mud all over me, and it was October and getting chilly. My team took me back to the hotel, where I put on a clean pair of shorts and—what the hell—kept drinking. When I woke up the next morning, my bed looked like a damn beach—sand was everywhere, I was bruised up on my side, and my wet clothes were piled in the corner of the room. All I could think about was how I did not want my wife, Faye, to see those dirty-ass clothes when I got home, so I put them in the back of my truck, thinking I'd take them out before she could see them. Well, I drove home and while I waited for Faye to get home from her job as the county tax commissioner, I got those muddy clothes and washed them, but I didn't have time to put them in the dryer. When Faye got home she went into the laundry room, then came back out and said, "When did you start washing clothes?" I said, "Honey, I know you work hard all day, and I didn't want you to have to work so hard at home, too," and I thought I'd just about get away with it. But then she said, "No, your muddy ass fell in the creek in Lynchburg!" Turns out someone emailed her a picture of the whole thing and she was just waiting for me to tell her about it—she already knew before I even got there. I'd like to tell you the whole mess happened because an anaconda crawled out of that creek and pulled me into it, but it's not true. I tumbled in like a wheel.

I love to tell that story on myself and I love the part about my wife outsmarting me, but the truth is I only drink after a cooking contest is over. I learned a long time ago that when it comes to competition barbecue, you can't win both the party on Friday night and the barbecue contest on Sunday—it's got to be one or the other, and I'm there to make my living, so there's no choice. Even one beer makes you less clearheaded and more likely to miss a crucial detail while you're cooking. The competition on the professional barbecue circuit is so tough nowadays that if you drink before you cook, you'll wind up losing. You've still got teams that go to contests to party and throw down, and they don't ever win a thing. Now I'm not saying that if you quit drinking it's going to make you a better pitmaster, but it's going to make you pay a lot more attention to what you're doing. You work hard, you focus hard, and once you're done you can let your hair down.

STEAKS

"Steak" ought to be synonymous with "Jack Mixon," because when my daddy wanted to do something nice for himself, he would eat a steak. He probably loved a T-bone more than he loved some members of his family. And he made sure he got one every weekend, too. Although a steak is a relatively small piece of tender meat compared to something like a hog shoulder, you can still smoke it in the pit with great success. It's true that grilling a steak over high heat can give you that seared-in crust on the outside with a moist, juicy center, but if you follow my method, you can produce the same result from pit cooking (it will take more time, of course, because you're cooking over lower heat) and your steak will taste different from any you've ever pulled off a grill.

RIB-EYE
STEAKS

I have been cooking steaks my whole life: The first meal my dad ever let me cook for my family was steak, so I know a thing or two about how it's done. There are two secrets to a great grilled steak. Number one: Buy the best quality of meat you can, because it really does make a difference when it comes to steaks. Number two: You need a golden, seared crust on that meat to lock in its juices and flavors. You get that crust by cooking the steak over dry heat on a very hot grill or in the pit by smoking it.

Cooking time: *Makes:*

ABOUT 50 MINUTES   **2 OR 3 SERVINGS PER STEAK**

ingredients

12- to 16-ounce (0.3- to 0.5-kg) bone-in rib-eye steaks (1½ inches / 4 cm thick)

Distilled white vinegar

Kosher salt and freshly ground black pepper

Pit Mop *(page 57)*

1: SELECT AND PREP THE MEAT
You need steaks that are at least 1½ inches (4 cm) thick and pref-erably thicker, and close to a pound (0.5 kg) each (remember you're serving them to more than one person), because steaks of this size and thickness do best in smokers.

Trim any excess fat from the steaks, taking care to leave a good ½ inch (12 mm) of fat around them to ensure you get a good crust. Spritz the steaks all over with white vinegar. Season them liberally with salt and pepper all over the fat and the meat.

2: PREPARE THE PIT OR SMOKER AND PUT THE MEAT ON *(see pages 41-51 for details)*
Gently set the steaks on the grate in the pit.

3: KEEP THE TEMP CONSISTENT, FLIP THE STEAKS, MOP THE STEAKS
Remember that we don't get a searing fire with these coals like you do on a grill, so it's going to take more time to cook the steaks. You want to maintain a temperature of about 275°F (135°C) in order to get a crispy bark on the outside of the meat. Cook the steaks for 15 minutes, then flip the steaks. We're going to go 15 minutes on the second side and then flip them again. Now we're going to cook for 10 minutes on the original side. Then we're going to flip them and go for 10 minutes more on the second side and then hit the steaks with our mop.

4: TEST FOR DONENESS

To test for doneness, press the top of the steak with your index finger: Rare will be soft and yielding; medium will be firmer; well-done steak will be quite firm. You can also use an instant-read thermometer inserted from the side. For medium rare, cook to 130 to 140°F (55 to 60°C); for medium, cook to 150°F (65°C); anything over 165°F (75°C) is well done, Jack Mixon–style.

5: PULL AND EAT THAT MEAT

Now we're going to bring the steaks out of the pit and transfer them to a wooden cutting board, cover with foil, and let them rest for 5 minutes. They're ready to eat. Perfect. You could almost cut them with a fork. But instead you're going to make thick slices cut against the grain and eat these with a big baked potato on the side.

ON THE GRILL
OR SMOKER

Prepare the steaks as described on *page 178*. About 30 minutes before you're ready to cook them, prepare a charcoal or gas grill or a smoker with a grate to 500°F (260°C). Place the steak on the grate or grill and sear it over direct heat for about 3 minutes per side. For rare, cook to 125°F (52°C); for medium-rare, cook to 145°F (63°C); for well done, look for a thermometer reading of "UGH!", which translates to anything over 165°F (75°C). Transfer the steaks to a platter and cover with foil. Let rest for 5 minutes. Uncover the steaks. The best way to carve the steaks is to use a sharp knife to cut the bone out completely (save it someplace for yourself for gnawing on later on), and then cut the meat across the grain in thick diagonal slices. Then knock yourself out.

JACK MIXON'S
T-BONE STEAK

As I said in the introduction *(see page 21),* a T-bone steak was the first thing my dad ever let me cook and that I remember barbecuing. He loved a T-bone above anything out there. I'm not that way: I like the T-bone mostly because it reminds me of him—but to me, the rib-eye is the better steak. But my dad loved a damn T-bone, and this recipe is for him.

Cooking time:

ABOUT 20 MINUTES

Makes:

ABOUT 2 SERVINGS PER STEAK

ingredients

12- to 16-ounce (0.3- to 0.5-kg) T-bone steaks (1½ inches / 4 cm thick)

Distilled white vinegar

Kosher salt and freshly ground black pepper

Pit Mop *(page 57)*

1: SELECT AND PREP THE MEAT

Spritz the steaks all over with white vinegar. Then season them liberally all over with salt and pepper.

2: PREPARE THE PIT OR SMOKER AND PUT THE MEAT ON *(see pages 41–51 for details)*

Bring the temperature to 265°F (130°C). Gently set the steaks on the grate in the pit.

3: KEEP THE TEMP CONSISTENT, FLIP THE STEAKS, MOP THE STEAKS

You're looking at about a 20-minute total cook time for these. You're going to come in after about 10 minutes, mop them down with that mop, flip them, and mop again. Cook for another 10 minutes.

4: TEST FOR DONENESS

To test for doneness, press the top of the steak with your index finger: Rare will be soft and yielding; medium will be firmer; well-done steak will be quite firm. You can also use an instant-read thermometer inserted from the side. For medium rare, cook to 130 to 140°F (55 to 60°C); for medium, cook to 150°F (65°C); anything over 165°F (75°C) is well done, Jack Mixon–style.

5: PULL AND EAT THOSE STEAKS

Pull the steaks off the pit, transfer to a wooden cutting board, cover loosely with foil, and let them rest for 10 minutes. Then get your damn baked potato and your momma's garlic bread ready to rock and roll with a little salad with Thousand Island on it, some sweet tea, you're done. Maybe some Smoked Blackberry Cobbler *(page 214)* later.

ON THE GRILL
OR SMOKER

Prepare the steaks as described on *page 185*. About 30 minutes before you're ready to cook them, prepare a charcoal or gas grill or a smoker with a grate to 500°F (260°C). Place the steak on the grate or grill and sear it over direct heat for about 3 minutes per side. Transfer the steaks to a platter and cover with foil. Let rest for 5 minutes. Uncover the steaks. The best way to carve the steaks is to use a sharp knife to cut the bone out completely (save it someplace for yourself for gnawing on later on), and then cut the meat across the grain in thick diagonal slices. Then knock yourself out.

A HELPING HAND

MY DADDY WAS a hard and tough man, but he did have a "helping hand" side. When we barbecued for our family events, he would be sure to give additional food to the old folks in our community. He loved to go fishing, and when he'd catch fish he would clean 'em and give 'em to his friends to enjoy. One Christmas he loaned—and by "loaned" I knew that meant "gave"—money to a friend of his to help his family, even though the truth of the matter was that old Jack didn't have cash to spare because those were tough times for us, too. My mama was fire-hot mad with him for doing it, but that's who he was.

Odd as it sounds, my dad was in a lot of ways nicer to friends than he was to family. Jack would overlook mess-ups from others that he would never tolerate from family. I guess it was that he expected more from blood than he did from others. He instilled the idea of doing things the "right way" in his family, and to this day I expect more out of my family than anyone else. I just also make sure that I do what I can to help my family folk succeed in everything they do.

My daddy believed the right way was usually the old-fashioned way of doing things. He loved everything old, and he believed the old way of doing things was always best. He was taught at an early age to barbecue on brick pits just like his dad and granddad had. He could have changed his ways and adapted to modern devices as he got older and plenty of other easier options became available, but he didn't. He yearned for the ways of the rural southern lifestyle he grew up with. It was a tough and primitive life, but he loved it. For example, we had fifteen acres of sugar cane and a three-roller power cane mill that was more than a hundred years old. We ground the cane into juice and boiled the juice down into syrup. This all took place in the fall and winter, while we were still barbecuing in pits every week. On top of that, Jack had a running sawmill that was also more than a hundred years old, which we used to custom-cut cypress lumber and shingles that we used and sold.

So Jack was always busy and he also didn't drink. I remember I came home late one Friday night when I was nineteen and I was a "little bit" drunk. Mama was up and rushed me off to bed so as not to wake Daddy. The next morning he got me up, took me down to the mill, and worked me all day long nonstop. He never mentioned drinking but he damn near killed my hungover ass. I never came home drunk again. (Not that I didn't drink, but when I did I knew to spend the night somewhere else.)

The deal with my dad is that he believed in the tried-and-true way of doing things, because you had to have skill, knowledge, and the drive to succeed. Whether it was cutting wood, making syrup, or cooking meat, he taught me how to do it "right." And he tried to make sure that's how I lived my life, too.

BEEF EXTRAS

If I thought it wouldn't be cheating barbecue fans out of their money, I might not bother to give you a burger recipe—these days you can get a "gourmet" burger just about any old place. The burger trend has spread far and wide, my friends, and you don't need me to tell you about it. But you know that special flavor that only comes from smoking meat in a pit? Wait until you try a burger smoked in that pit, and you'll forget about that so-called gourmet version that costs a week's salary. The "extra" things you can do with beef that I show you in this section elevate very common preparations—like meatloaf, tomato soup, and simple stock, in addition to the burgers—into intense and very flavorful foods, the kind folks remember long after they're eaten. You can use the smoked beef stock here as a base for any soup or sauce you like; it lends smoky richness to anything you add it to. Try boiling pasta with it sometime, and you'll see.

SMOKED
BURGERS

Like most red-blooded Americans, I like a burger. I've made hundreds if not thousands in my lifetime, and I've won prizes for cooking them. When I fire up my masonry pits, I will occasionally throw a burger or three in there because that smoke-kissed flavor cannot be beat—a burger smoked in the pit is even better than one on the grill because of that distinct flavor. If you've got your pit stoking, give it a try. It'll be the longest-cooked burger you've ever had, but it might just be the best.

Cooking time:	Makes:
ABOUT 20 MINUTES	**2 SERVINGS**

ingredients

1 pound (0.5 kg) ground beef

1½ teaspoons kosher salt

1½ teaspoons freshly ground black pepper

1 tablespoon Vinegar-Based Barbecue Sauce (page 55; optional), plus more for serving, if you like

Pit Mop (page 57)

2 hamburger buns, split

Toppings (optional): Lettuce, tomato slices, mayonnaise

If you can grind your own beef from good brisket, by all means do that. If you buy it, like most people, get some good local grass-fed beef if you can, and get some with some fat content in it—80/20 is ideal.

Every recipe you'll ever read for making burgers will tell you not to overhandle the ground beef or mush it up too much when you make your patties. I like a big-ass burger (I make two from a pound), and I like to mix a little barbecue sauce in with the meat. For the most basic burger: In a medium bowl, use your hands to gently combine the beef with the salt, pepper, and sauce, if using, until the seasonings are integrated with the beef. Form into two patties (or more if you want smaller burgers).

You want to put the burgers in the pit when it's running at about 300°F (150°C). Lay the burgers on the grate above the coals.

For medium rare, cook the burgers for 7 to 8 minutes, hit them with the mop, flip them, mop the top side, cook for 3 to 4 minutes more, and then serve.

To test for doneness, insert an instant-read thermometer from the side of a burger into the center. The internal temperature should be about 145°F (63°C) for medium rare.

Pull the burgers from the pit and let them rest, lightly covered with foil, on a wooden cutting board or a platter for about 10 minutes. Toast your buns, set up your lettuce, tomatoes, and mayo and your barbecue sauce and whatever else you like on your burger, and chow down.

IN THE SMOKER

PREP:

Prepare your smoker to 300°F (150°C). Prepare your burgers as directed on the opposite page, forming one pound of ground beef into two patties (again, form more if you want smaller burgers). Place the burgers in a shallow aluminum pan, and place the pan in the smoker.

COOK:

Cook for 15 minutes for medium-rare, and up to 30 minutes for medium-well. Remove the burgers from the smoker and allow them to rest, uncovered, while you melt 2 tablespoons of cold unsalted butter in a medium skillet over medium heat. When the butter is hot (but not smoking), slide the burgers carefully into the skillet using a spatula. Cook the burgers for about 3 minutes on each side, just until they're seared and a nice crust has formed (taking care not to overcook them). Top the patties with slices of cheddar cheese, if you like. Slide the burgers onto a platter and let them rest, lightly covered with aluminum foil, while you toast a couple of buns on the "light" setting in a toaster oven or toaster.

EAT:

Fill the buns with the burgers and top with whatever you like; for me, it's a light smear of mayonnaise, a slice of ripe tomato, and a nice piece of iceberg lettuce. And that's a damn good burger.

BONE, TOMATO & ONION
SOUP

When I was growing up with my family we didn't think we were poor, but looking back I realize that by most standards we probably were. So anytime we'd get a steak we didn't waste anything on it. Since my dad loved T-bones and that's what we mostly ate when we could, my grandmother took the leftover bones, some tomatoes, and onions we had in the garden and made this soup.

My granny, who we lived with until I was ten years old, never did eat steak herself. She waited until we were done eating and she took our bones away. I loved my granny to death, but she was the one that made my daddy as tough and ornery as he was—he took after her, which, come to think of it, wasn't a bad thing. If my dad had been any less strict with me I might not have learned all these lessons about barbecue that I'm trying to pass on to you.

Cooking time:

ABOUT 3½ HOURS

Makes:

6 TO 8 SERVINGS

ingredients

4 or 5 T-bone steak bones or other steak bones

Distilled white vinegar

Kosher salt and freshly ground black pepper

2 cups (240 g) thinly sliced onions

12 small tomatoes, diced

Rinse the bones thoroughly in cold water and pat them dry with a clean kitchen towel or paper towels. Wipe them down with a little white vinegar. Season the bones with salt and pepper. In a large heavy soup pot or Dutch oven, submerge the steak bones in 5 cups (1.2 L) water. Add the onions. Season the water with additional salt and pepper to taste. Bring to a boil over high heat, reduce the heat to medium, and boil for 30 minutes.

Add the tomatoes, reduce the heat, and let the soup gently simmer over low heat, stirring occasionally, for 2½ to 3 hours, until the soup has a rich meaty flavor and the tomatoes have disintegrated. Taste the soup occasionally for seasoning and add more salt and pepper as needed. Remove from the heat and skim off any fat that has risen to the surface. Strain the liquid into a clean pot and discard the bones. Serve this soup piping hot with some crusty bread or buttered rolls on the side, if you like.

SMOKED
BEEF STOCK

Smoking in your pit today? Might as well throw some bones in there, smoke them, and make stock. You can use this as the base for just about any soup or stew or sauce (it's an especially good base for tomato soup). It's handy to have around, and it's got much more flavor than anything you can buy at the grocery store in a can. Many grocery stores sell beef bones in the freezer section near the meat department, but you can buy the bones from a butcher, too.

Cooking time:

ABOUT 6 HOURS

Makes:

ABOUT 8 CUPS

ingredients

5 pounds (2.3 kg) beef or veal marrow bones

Distilled white vinegar

Kosher salt and freshly ground black pepper

1 large yellow onion

2 large carrots, peeled and coarsely chopped

2 stalks celery, including leaves, cut into thirds

1 large tomato

1 medium potato, scrubbed and cut into 1-inch (2.5-cm) cubes

4 sprigs fresh parsley, or 2 teaspoons dried parsley

1 bay leaf

2 teaspoons dried thyme

2 cloves garlic, peeled and smashed

1 egg white

1 crushed eggshell

Wash your bones in cold water and dry them. Spritz them all over with white vinegar, and season them with salt and pepper. Put them in a heavy baking pan or aluminum baking pan in a single layer. Put the pan in the pit and smoke with whatever else you've got smoking in the pit at 250 to 300°F (120 to 150°C) for 5 hours. Remove them from the pit, cover the pan with foil, and let them cool completely, about 1 hour.

In a large heavy soup pot or Dutch oven, combine the smoked bones with the onion, carrots, celery, tomato, potato, herbs, garlic, 1 tablespoon salt, and 12 cups (2.8 L) water. Over medium-high heat, bring to a boil. Reduce the heat to low and gently simmer, stirring occasionally, for 5 hours. After 5 hours, remove from the heat and let the stock cool to room temperature, about 30 minutes. Using a cheesecloth-lined colander, strain the stock into a clean pot. Discard the solids.

Clarify the stock to remove solid flecks that remain in the stock but that are too small to be strained out with cheesecloth: In a small bowl combine ¼ cup (60 ml) cold water with the egg white and eggshell and stir together to combine. Add the mixture to the pot with the strained stock. Bring to a boil over medium-high heat. As soon as the stock boils, remove it from the heat and let it stand for 10 minutes, until slightly cooled. Strain again through a sieve lined with cheesecloth and discard the solids. Transfer the stock to airtight containers. Refrigerate for at least 8 hours, or overnight; when ready to use, skim off the fat that collects on top of the stock (it is much easier to do this when the stock is cold). The stock can be refrigerated for up to 3 days or frozen for up to 4 months.

SMOKED
MEATLOAF

I enjoy meatloaf tremendously, and it's best when smoked in a pit. Sometimes I make it meatball-style, other times I make it like the traditional loaf. Lots of people make meatloaf with bread crumbs, but I make cracker crumbs with buttery Ritz crackers. The smoky flavor of this pit-cooked meatloaf is unmistakable. If you've got your pit going, you're probably making lots of meat, but throw a meatloaf in there, smoke it, and save it for meatloaf sandwiches for your weekday lunches. That's how to use a pit with some planning.

Cooking time:	Makes:
ABOUT 2 HOURS	**1 (9-INCH / 23-CM) MEATLOAF, ABOUT 6 SERVINGS**

ingredients

Butter or nonstick cooking spray, for the pan

½ cup (120 ml) buttermilk

1 cup (240 ml) Vinegar-Based Barbecue Sauce (page 55)

1 cup (60 g) finely crushed Ritz crackers (about 20 crackers)

1 pound (0.5 kg) ground beef, 80% lean

1 pound (0.5 kg) ground pork

½ teaspoon freshly grated nutmeg

½ cup grated Parmigiano-Reggiano cheese

1 large egg, beaten

1 tablespoon barbecue rub (your favorite brand, or I'll sell you one of mine at jacksoldsouth.com)

Kosher salt and freshly ground black pepper

Pit Mop (page 57)

Grease a 9 x 5-inch (23 x 12-cm) loaf pan or a 10 x 6-inch (25 x 15-cm) baking dish with butter or nonstick cooking spray.

In a large bowl, whisk the buttermilk with the barbecue sauce. Stir in the crackers, beef, pork, nutmeg, cheese, egg, rub, salt, and pepper and mix well. Pack the mixture into the prepared pan. Cover the pan with foil.

You want your pit temperature to be between 250 and 300°F (120 and 150°C), which it will be if you're smoking any of our big meats. Place the meatloaf in the pit on the grate over the coals and smoke for 1 hour. Uncover the meatloaf and brush your vinegar mop on top of it. Cook for 30 minutes more, then hit it again with the mop. At the 2-hour mark, insert an instant-read thermometer into the center of the meatloaf; when the meatloaf registers 150°F (65°C), remove it from the pit, transfer the pan to a heatproof surface, and allow it to rest, loosely covered with foil, for 20 minutes before slicing and serving.

IN THE SMOKER

The total cooking time of the meatloaf will depend on the heat of your fire and the size of your baking pan or dish, but expect about 3 hours. Prepare the meatloaf as directed on the opposite page. Prepare an offset smoker with soaked wood chips and heat it up to 350°F (175°C). When the smoker is ready, place the meatloaf pan on the cool side of the smoker. Cover the smoker and cook the meatloaf until its temperature registers 140°F (60°C); start checking the temperature at the 2-hour mark and keep checking every 15 minutes after that. At the 140°F (60°C) mark, brush ¼ cup (60 ml) Pit Mop *(page 57)* on top of the meatloaf and put it back on the smoker. The sauce will set into a shiny glaze while the meatloaf reaches its final temperature of 150 to 160°F (65 to 71°C). Once there, transfer the meatloaf pan to a heatproof surface, cover it with foil, and allow it to rest for 20 minutes before slicing and serving.

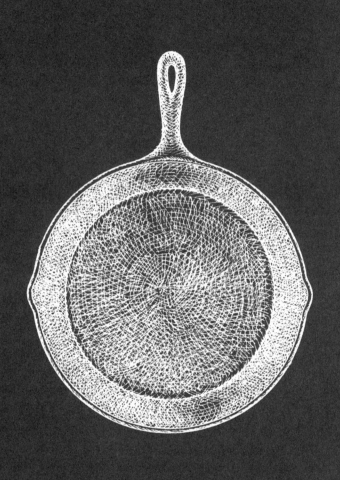

CHAPTER 5:

EXTRAS

EXTRAS

I preach to folks who are interested in learning how to cook old-school barbecue on coal-fired masonry pits that when they fire up their pits, they should take advantage of the situation and cook as much as they can. Make hay while the sun shines, if you like. And I practice what I preach. When I fire up my pit, you'll likely find me cooking up some of my favorite pit-flavored sides that I remember from my childhood, like smoked hoop cheese (never heard of it? Turn to *page 208* to enlighten yourself—you'll thank me later) and smoked trout. And I'm also going to share with you some of my granny's formulas for pulled candy and soap, both of which are old-school recipes from days gone by that evoke the pit-smoking lifestyle at its best.

SMOKED
SALT

As far as rubs and seasonings go, the way I learned to barbecue was with just two ingredients: salt and pepper. And in this book I wanted to return to this most basic of formulas. It's so simple I wonder if everybody will say, "He just wants us to use salt and pepper?" And I will answer that for this style of pit cooking, it's adequate. It's more than damn adequate. But if you want to use your favorite rub, I can't stop you. I've got a bunch of rub recipes that I could give you and I also sell my own brand of rubs; when I do competitions, I use those. But I don't use that stuff when I cook in my pits. At the end of the day, simple is better. The smoky flavor the pit emits is powerful, so it's best to stick to salt and pepper and not mess too much with it. One way I have of extending that smoky flavor to other foods is through something I figured out that not even my dad knew about: smoked salts. If you have smoked salt in your pantry, you're ahead of the game before you even start cooking.

The process of infusing wood smoke into your salt is very easy to do in the coal-fired pits, but you can also do it on your regular smoker at home.

Cooking time:	Makes:
5 HOURS	**ABOUT 2 CUPS (440 G)**

ingredients

About 2 cups (480 g) salt
(kosher or plain iodized,
whatever you prefer; enough
to cover the bottom of a
cookie sheet)

The best time to smoke your salt is when you're cooking something for a long time in the smoker and it's going to be maintaining a steady temperature. Pour a layer of salt about ½ inch (12 mm) deep onto a large (13 x 18-inch / 33 x 46-cm) rimmed cookie sheet. Smooth it down carefully so that it's in as even a layer as you can arrange it, and put it on the opposite side of the smoker from whatever meat you've got on there, then fire that pit for about 5 hours. By doing this, you're going to infuse the salt with the smoke (in my case it's going to be a combination of the hickory and oak woods flavoring the salt). You can take a lot of recipes in this book and substitute smoked salt for the kosher salt I call for, and you can also add that smoked salt to vegetables and other meats, too. After 5 hours, remove the pan from the pit, let the salt cool to room temperature, and store it in a jar.

SMOKED
HOOP CHEESE

Hoop cheese is an old southern staple that you can barely find in the South anymore. It was traditionally made by farmers from cow's milk that had been drained entirely of its whey; the remaining curd was poured into a round mold, aka the hoop, and pressed—the cheese is usually semisoft. It used to be made in-house in small-town grocery stores, where it was cut fresh from big wheels. Sometimes it's called "red-rind cheese" for obvious reasons; it has a mild flavor and very creamy texture. (Ashe County Cheese, in the mountain town of West Jefferson, North Carolina, can ship you some if you can't find it locally: www.ashecountycheese.com.)

Cooking time:	*Makes:*
2 TO 4 HOURS	**1 POUND (0.5 KG)**

ingredients

1 (1-pound / 0.5-kg) wheel of hoop cheese

You want to set up your smoker precisely as you would to cook all your meats, but we want it even lower: You want a heat of about 140°F (60°C), and you want to put a few hot coals on one side, and the cheese on the side without the coals. Remember, we're not trying to cook the cheese or even melt it; we just want to get some good smoky flavor on it.

Take your hoop cheese and place it on a cookie sheet or in a shallow aluminum pan (you can do more than one round if you like). Set the sheet in the smoker and smoke the cheese for 2 to 4 hours, depending on about how much smoke you want on the cheese. If you go 2 hours, the cheese will be firmer and you'll have the flavor of smoke on it—you can slice it for sandwiches or eat it on crackers this way and it's delicious. If you go the full 4 hours, it will be quite soft, creamy, very melty, and very smoky, and in this state you can stir it into some pasta or use it to top nachos—the flavor will be strong and the consistency will be on the softer side.

SMOKED
WHOLE TROUT

My dad loved to fish, and we spent a lot of time doing that when I was growing up; it was his real passion—he loved it even more than barbecue. Trout is one of my favorite fish to cook and eat because it's hardy enough to stand up to the smoking process, so when I'm firing up my pit for other meats, I know I can throw in some trout and then eat the smoked trout on crackers for a quick app, in a sandwich for lunch, or mixed with a little sour cream and mayonnaise for the world's most delicious smoky dip.

Cooking time:

30 MINUTES TO 1 HOUR

Makes:

4 SERVINGS

ingredients

½ cup (120 g) kosher salt, plus more for seasoning

2 pounds (0.9 kg) trout fillets (4 to 6 ounces / 115 to 170 g each), skin on, pin bones removed

Distilled white vinegar

Freshly ground black pepper

In a heavy medium pot, combine the salt with 4 cups (1 L) water over medium-high heat and bring to a boil, stirring to dissolve the salt. Remove from the heat and let cool to room temperature, about 30 minutes. Submerge the trout fillets in the brine, cover, and refrigerate until ready to use, at least 30 minutes or up to 3 hours.

During this time you should be setting up your pit and getting some meat on there, so you have it at 250°F (120°C) when you're ready to cook your trout.

Remove the trout from the brine and rinse the fillets thoroughly in fresh cold water. Spritz the trout with white vinegar and season it with salt and pepper. Put the trout in an aluminum pan in a single layer, skin side down, with at least ½ inch (12 mm) of space between the fillets, and put the pan on the grate in the pit. Smoke the trout for 30 minutes to 1 hour, until the fish is cooked through, flakes easily when prodded with a fork, and has darkened in color from transparent white to pearly white. Remove the trout from the smoker and serve immediately.

OLD-FASHIONED
PULLED CANDY

I have many memories of my granny pulling candy by our sugar-processing shack; she would pull it and pull it and my mouth would water and water. I associate it with pit cooking because it's the same kind of old-school real southern technique that's simple and cheap to do and turns into something delicious to eat. You can see folks pulling candy at the beach towns in the South to this day, like in Myrtle Beach and Panama City, where they make saltwater taffy, which is similar to this candy.

Makes:

ABOUT 3 DOZEN SMALL CANDIES

ingredients

1¼ cups (300 ml) sorghum syrup or dark molasses

¾ cup (150 g) sugar

1 tablespoon distilled white vinegar

1 tablespoon unsalted butter

⅛ teaspoon baking soda

⅛ teaspoon kosher salt

A few drops peppermint oil or chopped walnuts *(optional)*

Butter a glass 9 x 13-inch (23 x 33-cm) lasagna dish and set aside.

In a large heavy pot over medium heat, combine the sorghum or molasses with the sugar and vinegar and, stirring occasionally to prevent burning, cook until the mixture reaches 270°F (132°C) on a candy thermometer, the soft-crack stage. Remove from the heat and add the butter, baking soda, and salt and stir just enough to blend. Pour the candy into the prepared pan. When cool enough to handle, after about 5 minutes, gather the mixture into a ball and pull it between your ungreased fingertips until the candy is a firm, light-colored strip. Cut it into 1-inch (2.5-cm) pieces and wrap each in waxed paper.

You can add a few drops of peppermint oil or some chopped walnuts to the candy before pulling, if you like.

SMOKED
CORNBREAD

This is a no-brainer when it comes to a side dish that you can throw into the pit while you're smoking your big meats. I make up a batch of skillet cornbread and set that sucker down in my pit for it to acquire the unmistakable flavor only a coal-fired pit smoker can give. This cornbread cooks at just about the same temp that most meats cook (250 to 300°F / 120 to 150°C); check your temperature regularly and keep it as consistent as you can.

Cooking time:	Makes:
ABOUT 45 MINUTES	**1 (10-INCH / 25-CM) ROUND CORNBREAD**

ingredients

Unsalted butter, for the skillet

1 cup (180 g) yellow corn-meal, fine or medium-coarse grind

1 cup (125 g) all-purpose flour, sifted

2 tablespoons sugar

4 teaspoons baking powder

½ teaspoon kosher salt

1 large egg

1 cup (240 ml) buttermilk

⅓ cup (75 ml) sour cream

¼ cup (60 ml) vegetable oil

Grease a 10-inch (25-cm) cast-iron skillet with butter and set aside.

In a large bowl, combine the cornmeal, flour, sugar, baking powder, and salt and stir well. In a medium bowl, whisk together the egg, buttermilk, sour cream, and oil. Make a well in the center of the dry ingredients and pour in the egg mixture. Using a mixing spoon, stir together until well combined; the batter should have no lumps. Pour the batter into the prepared skillet.

Gently place the skillet in the pit and cook, maintaining the temperature at 250 to 300°F (120 to 150°C), until a skewer inserted into the center of the cornbread comes out clean, about 45 minutes. Remove from the smoker and let cool for 10 minutes on a wire rack. You can serve the cornbread warm out of the skillet if you like, or invert it onto a platter and let it cool to room temperature.

SMOKED
BLACKBERRY
COBBLER

Blackberries are my favorite fruit; when they're in season you can spot me carrying around pints of them for snacking as I check my smoker and pit temps. Something about that tart flavor with a little bit of sweetness to it gets me every time. Of course you can use this pancakelike topping over other fruits, too. In the South we like our desserts made with lard, and since we're cooking whole hogs in our pit, we have access to very high-quality fresh lard. You can also buy lard from good butcher shops, or substitute vegetable shortening if you prefer. This is something to make when your smoker is going and cooking meat in it.

Cooking time:	Makes:
ABOUT 1½ HOURS	**6 TO 8 SERVINGS**

ingredients

2 pints (560 g) fresh or frozen blackberries

¾ cup (150 g) granulated sugar

½ cup (110 g) firmly packed brown sugar

1 tablespoon plus ½ cup (65 g) all-purpose flour

1 tablespoon apple cider vinegar

1 teaspoon ground cinnamon

1 teaspoon baking powder

½ teaspoon kosher salt

½ cup (120 ml) buttermilk or whole milk

¼ cup (60 ml) lard or vegetable shortening

Vanilla ice cream, for serving (optional)

In a medium nonreactive bowl, stir together the blackberries, ¼ cup (50 g) of the granulated sugar, the brown sugar, 1 table-spoon of the flour, the vinegar, and the cinnamon. Set aside.

In another medium nonreactive bowl, sift together the remaining ½ cup (65 g) flour, the remaining ½ cup (100 g) granulated sugar, the baking powder, and the salt. Pour in the buttermilk and use a wooden spoon to stir and combine. The batter should be the consistency of pancake batter; it is fine if there are a few lumps. Set it aside.

In a 10-inch (25-cm) cast-iron skillet, melt the lard over medium heat until it starts to brown around the edge and foam. It should be sizzling; you should hear it. When you hear that lard start to brown and sizzle, pour the batter into the hot skillet. Do not stir it. Pour the fruit mixture right on top of the batter. Remove the skillet from the heat.

Transfer the skillet into the pit that you've been steadily maintaining at 250°F (120°C). Smoke the cobbler until the crust is golden and crisp-edged, about 1½ hours. Serve topped with vanilla ice cream, if you like.

SMOKED
CHOCOLATE
SKILLET CAKE

This is a great dessert to make at the end of your pit cooking, when your pit is hot and you want to get the most out of it that you can. This cake needs a slightly higher temp than most meats, though, so if you've been running the smoker at 250 to 300°F (120 to 150°C), you need to get it up to 325 to 350°F (165 to 175°C) to cook this cake. The rest is easy.

Cooking time:

45 MINUTES TO 1 HOUR

Makes:

10 TO 12 SERVINGS

ingredients

¾ cup (1½ sticks / 170 g) plus 1 tablespoon unsalted butter, softened

2 cups (250 g) all-purpose flour

½ cup (50 g) unsweetened cocoa powder

2 teaspoons baking powder

½ teaspoon baking soda

½ teaspoon kosher salt

1 cup (200 g) plus 2 tablespoons sugar

3 large eggs

3 ounces (85 g) semisweet chocolate, melted and cooled

2 teaspoons pure vanilla extract

1½ cups (360 ml) sour cream

Whipped cream and fresh fruit for serving (optional)

Generously grease an 8-cup (2-L) cast-iron skillet with 1 tablespoon of the butter and set aside.

In a medium bowl, sift the flour with the cocoa powder, baking powder, baking soda, and salt. In a large bowl using an electric mixer, beat the remaining ¾ cup (170 g) butter until creamy. Add the sugar and beat until light and fluffy. Add the eggs, one at a time, beating well after each addition. Add the melted chocolate and the vanilla and beat until the batter is smooth. Beat in the dry ingredients in three batches, alternating with the sour cream.

Scrape the batter into the prepared pan and use a rubber spatula to smooth the surface.

Place the skillet in the pit and cook for 45 minutes to 1 hour. Take special care to check the temperature every 10 minutes and maintain it between 325 and 350°F (165 to 175°C), shoveling in fresh hot coals as necessary. Smoke the cake until a skewer inserted into the center comes out with moist crumbs attached but no wet batter. Remove from the pit and let the cake cool completely in the pan on a rack, about 1 hour.

When ready to eat, invert the cake onto a serving platter. Cut it into wedges and serve with freshly whipped cream and fresh fruit (such as my favorite, blackberries), if you like.

I love chocolate cake and I love spareribs—
but I don't necessarily want my spareribs to taste like

CHOCOLATE CAKE.

I will throw a chocolate cake in my pit at the end of a big cook, though.

PIT ASH LYE

Homemade soap is something my granny made because like a lot of southern people she couldn't get to the store all the time to buy it. I think it's as good a cleanser as any commercial soap, nice and gentle on your skin, and especially good to use if you have poison ivy or bug bites. The alkaline properties of lye soap neutralize and break down the bug's stinging saliva, which means that the bite is less likely to be itchy and painful in the hours and days that follow. Most soap is made from lye, the chemical used in cleaning products that is highly soluble in water. What is lye made of? It's made from leaching ashes, exactly the kind of ashes that come from hardwood (oak, hickory, maple, and so on) and fruit woods (apple, peach, cherry, and so on). So after you've fired up your pit and smoked all your food in it, you can take the ashes and make yourself some soap just like my granny did.

A note about lye: There are two types. Homemade lye is potassium hydroxide and can be made at home from wood ashes mixed with fat or oils such as beef tallow or pig lard. You can use other fats such as olive oil or coconut oil or avocado oil in place of the animal fat, if you like. Commercial lye, available in some grocery stores and most hardware stores, is sodium hydroxide, which is more caustic than the homemade kind and makes a less appealing soap. Besides, this is a barbecue book and I'm not going to tell you to go to the store and buy lye if you have perfectly good ashes to work with when you're done cooking. Both types are strong chemicals that can cause burns and quickly eat through many materials (including skin), so do wear gloves and protective eyewear for this process.

Add-ins: I'm giving you a basic soap method, but there are many additions you can include if you like: Colorings, herbs, flowers, honey, oatmeal, and essential oils are all good examples.

To make a reasonable quantity of lye, you will need 2 gallons (7.6 L) of wood ashes. You are looking for white, paperlike ashes; not black or gray chunks of charcoallike wood.

Makes:

4 (1/4-POUND / 2-KG) BARS OF SOAP

materials & tools

Two 5-gallon (19-L) plastic buckets (or similarly sized wooden barrels; do not use aluminum or metal, which the solution will corrode)

2 gallons (7.6 L) white wood ash

About 3 gallons (11 L) water (rainwater or spring water work best because their mineral content is lower than that of tap water, but tap water will work fine)

Apron

Rubber gloves

Plastic sunglasses or other plastic protective eyewear

Cheesecloth and plastic colander

Deep and wide waterproof container (to go under the bucket)

Egg or small potato

Heavy cooking pots

1 pound (0.5 kg) lard, beef tallow, or other animal fat

Wooden spoon

About ½ cup (120 g) kosher salt *(optional; for bar soap)*

1) MAKE THE LYE WATER: Wearing your apron, gloves, and protective eyewear, collect about 2 gallons (7.6 L) white ash from the pit in one of the buckets—a little less than half of the bucket's capacity. Be sure to choose the thinnest, most papery ashes and no black chunks of coal. Pour in 1 gallon (3.8 L) water. Cover the container and let the solution settle for about 3 hours.

2) WEARING YOUR APRON, gloves, and protective eyewear, use cheesecloth and a plastic colander to strain the lye water solution into the second bucket. You can place a deep and wide waterproof container under the bucket to catch any spills (not pictured here).

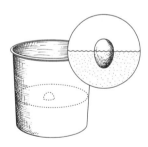

3) DO THE EGG / POTATO TEST to determine if the solution is concentrated enough to make soap: Float an egg or potato in the solution. When the solution has the right amount of concentration, the egg or small potato will float so that about ½ to 1 inch (12 mm to 2.5 cm) of it remains above the water's surface. If it sinks, the solution is too weak and you should boil the lye water down, reducing it by about a third, letting it cool, and trying the test again by repeating the process of pouring the lye water over the ashes again along with 2 gallons (7.6 L) fresh water, letting it settle for 3 hours, re-straining, and trying again until the water supports the egg correctly. When the solution is right, discard the ashes. If it floats

and turns sideways, it is too strong; add water to the solution 1 cup (240 ml) at time, repeating the test until the water supports the egg correctly.

4) PREPARE THE FAT: You can obtain the animal fat from a good butcher; ask for beef tallow or pork lard. Or you can render it yourself: Remove about 1 cup (240 ml) of the fat from the meat you've smoked (such as a whole hog or brisket) and melt it slowly over low heat in a large frying pan. Once thoroughly melted, strain the grease through cheesecloth into a heavy medium pot. Combine an equal amount of water with the strained grease, bring to a boil over medium heat, add ¼ cup (60 ml) fresh cold water, remove from the heat, and let cool. Once the fat hardens in the pot, scrape off any parts that look "dirty" or dark, and remove the hardened fat from the water to store in a dry container.

5) MAKE THE SOAP: You should have 1 pound (0.5 kg) lard and 1⅔ to 2 gallons (6.3 to 7.6 L) lye water. In a medium pot over medium heat, melt the lard. Transfer this to a large heavy container (plastic or wood, not metal) and combine it with the lye water, stirring with a wooden spoon. Once the mixture has a creamy, light caramel appearance, test it for doneness: Place a small dab of the soap on a glass or china plate and let it cool for 20 minutes. If it's done the cooled mixture will appear transparent with white streaks and specks throughout. If it is gray and weak looking or has a gray margin, it needs more lye. If it cools with a gray skin over it, it needs more fat. You can reheat what you've got in your container, the fat-and-lye-water mixture, and adjust as necessary. You can pour it into any liquid soap container to use at this point.

6) IF YOU WANT BAR SOAP, you need to reduce the soap's water content. Adding the salt will separate the soap and the water. Once the salt is added, let the mixture cool completely. During this time the soap will separate from the water and float on top. Remove the soap to a heavy medium pot, add a small amount of water (no more than ½ cup / 120 ml), and bring to a boil; boil for 5 to 6 minutes, then skim the soap from the surface. Using a kitchen towel or mitts to protect your hands, you can pour the liquid soap into a mold—small silicone breadstick molds are great for this—or other square plastic molds in the shape of bars of soap—and let it cool and harden, then remove from the mold.

LIFE, DEATH, *and* BARBECUE

BESIDES ME, THE greatest pitmaster of all time probably would be my dad, because he actually knew how to cook without any damn gadgets or technology. In terms of folks who cook barbecue for a living, you have a lot of unsung heroes in this game and a lot of people who never got any notoriety. To be recognized as a great pitmaster today you have to be a great showman. I'm not saying that that's right, but it's a fact: We live in a world now where media rules. Everything now is so instant, you gotta be that guy or gal who not only can cook but also can relay that message to the public.

I'll tell you a story about my public life. I was inducted into the Barbecue Hall of Fame in 2013 at the Royal in Kansas City, one of the most prestigious competitions in barbecue. That's the best thing that's ever happened to me, because you're voted in by your peers who are other barbecue people. My induction ceremony was for pitmaster, and I gave credit to my dad. It's been a long path to get to where I am today, but my dad got me started, and Pat Burke was the guy I chased who showed me how to be a champion.

So according to the world I'm a champion pitmaster. But this book is all about how "pitmaster" means something different today than it did in my daddy's day. Sometimes I wonder what old Jack would think about what a pitmaster has come to mean and about how barbecuing is something that is now associated with fame and fortune. His idea of a pitmaster was like one from two hundred years ago, when the pitmaster in the community was a guy of importance, the keeper of the fire. That was the guy who cooked for the reunions and cooked the thirty hogs for the churches and for the governor coming around and stumping for the state. It wasn't anything like competition barbecue.

Competition meat is a totally different genre of food than what you would call authentic barbecue. The comp meat is good, but for me, if I'm going to sit down and eat a plate of barbecue, I want to eat what I was raised eating. It's not about nostalgia, but you taste the meat, you taste the vinegar, you taste the smoke—and that's it. Competition barbecue is so rich, it's so heavy with flavor that you take one bite and that's about all you can stand. Pitmasters know how to keep it simple. And their stakes are higher: If you lose a competition, it's not the end of the world. For my dad, who cooked seventy-five joints of meat every week, if he screwed up one pit full of meat he screwed up three days' worth of sales—don't forget there's a lot of labor involved in barbecue because you have to do the prep work, clean the pit, feed and stoke the pit, hold that meat to a consistent temperature . . . I learned how to do that though trial and error. My dad didn't allow mistakes, and he sold every damn bit of that meat every week.

I don't have a restaurant like he did. I have competitions, though. The first time someone wins a trophy is fun; it's a great feeling because winning is a great thing. But the best thing for me is the people I've met, great cooks like Art Smith and Tuffy Stone. If it hadn't been for competition barbecue, I wouldn't have known them. Competition barbecue has also brought me closer to my brother, Tracy, which is something I didn't think would happen and couldn't have envisioned. Barbecue has been good for my family, and it's provided a living that I wouldn't have been able to make any other way. I feel like the luckiest man in the world. I ain't saying I don't have skills in barbecue, but I was lucky: I was at the right place at the right time when barbecue took off nationally as something that was bigger than people's backyards. I was already there, doing my thing. Some people peak too early, but I was still rocking and rolling in my prime (I still think I'm in my prime). My dad didn't think a lot about competition barbecue. In fact, he thought it was kind of silly and for folks who didn't have to worry about making a living. *If he could see me now*, I think sometimes.

You never know what is going to happen at a contest, and in that way it's a lot like life. Recently I was cooking at a contest down in Bainbridge, Georgia, and there were seventy-five teams, including all the top-ten Kansas City BBQ Society contenders. The contest had a lot of money in it; the grand champion had a $7,500 prize. A perfect score in a category was 180 points. (In my life, I've gotten three 180s, two of them at the Jack Daniel's Invitational for whole hog, one at a contest in Dillard, Georgia, for ribs.) This guy who had driven down to Georgia from New Jersey got a 180 for chicken. Then he went back to his tent and died of a massive heart attack. Got a 180 and passed away. He was only in his midfifties, and this was one of the happiest times of his life, and he goes and gets a perfect 180, puts it out on Facebook, calls his wife, he's so happy, and then he dies. Kind of puts things in perspective, don't it?

PIT TOOLS

This book is the opposite of one that is all about stuff you need to buy in order to make good barbecue. Remember that the thing I most want you to do is build a masonry pit—if you can do that, your life will be changed, my friends. That said, I understand that I use certain tools that you might want to make sure you have around because they make cooking over a coal-fired masonry pit (or another live and active heat source) that much easier. Here are the tools I suggest having that you should plan to use when you make my kind of barbecue:

Plastic work gloves for handling and prepping raw meat

Aluminum foil pans for transporting meat on and off the pit (take care to use a new one every time so you don't contaminate cooked meat with raw meat; disposability is key)

Plastic table coverings for meat prep

Plain old-fashioned wood-handled mops with long string (plan to saw off the handles to whichever length is most comfortable for you)

Coolers (to store meat while brining)

Plastic spray bottles for blasting meats with vinegar at prep time

Very good steel-forged knives (if you're going to splurge on something, it should be these because they will last a lifetime—I still use some knives that were my daddy's—but make sure you sharpen them regularly and treat them with care); I recommend at least three: a long chef's knife (10 to 12 inches / 25 to 30.5 cm); a paring knife; and a carving knife

Heavy wooden cutting boards (for letting meat rest and for slicing)

Tongs in varying lengths and sizes, springloaded (the best for manipulating meat on pits and smokers)

An instant-read meat thermometer (if you can't bear not to know the exact temp of your meat)

Heavy-duty leather or other durable work gloves for handling the pit when it's hot

A heavy garden hoe for raking coals

SELECTION & PREP

Here's my "just facts" version of how to get the main barbecue meats ready to go for the pit or smoker. You still need to consult the recipes in this book for the exact methods, but you can use this section for quick reference on how to prep these meats to get yourself and your barbecue going.

RIBS

For pork ribs: Spareribs, also called St. Louis ribs, are the long bones situated behind the shoulders and are from the lower part of the hog belly; they are straight and fatty, and the racks usually weigh about 4 pounds (1.8 kg) or less. When you buy them, look for ribs with meat that covers the whole bone—try to find racks where no rib bones are showing through the meat. Don't buy spares that are covered entirely in fat—there's often no meat on there to enjoy after you've finished cooking them.

For beef ribs: The secret to making what I call "tenderlicious" beef ribs, aka dinosaur bones (called that because they're so big), is that you don't have to do too much—these ribs are so tender because they sit right below the rib roast of the cow, which has lots of good marbling.

For both kinds of ribs: Fresh ribs that have never been frozen are best if you can find them. To trim them up before pit-smoking them, place them on a clean cutting board, bone side down. The first three ribs are the fattiest: Use a sharp knife to trim off the excess fat surrounding these. Then turn the slab over; you'll see that there's a thick, clear-white membrane covering the backs of the ribs. You want to pull this membrane off because it makes the ribs tough to chew, but you need to do it with a combination of gentle-yet-firm pulling. First make a small incision just below the length of the breastbone. Work your fingers underneath the membrane until you have 2 to 3 inches (5 to 7.5 cm) cleared. Grab the membrane with a towel or other clean cloth and gently but firmly pull it away from the ribs. Pulling off the membrane exposes loose fat, so after you've discarded the membrane, go in with your paring knife and trim any excess exposed fat. Use a clean towel to pat the ribs try. Then apply white vinegar all over both sides of the rack, and season all over with salt and pepper.

PORK SHOULDER

A pork shoulder has two parts: the lower ("arm") piece, commonly called the "picnic," and the upper piece, commonly called the "Boston butt." These are just

names for cuts that have evolved in the vernacular lingo of cooks and butchers over time. When you want to cook a pork shoulder, look for one that is well marbled (shot through with visible fat) and as squared-up and regularly shaped as an irregular-looking piece of meat can be (you're thinking about consistent and even cooking time, so try to find a shoulder without too many lumps and bumps).

A pork shoulder can be an unwieldy piece of meat but it's very easy to master. First, place the shoulder on a clean large cutting board and use a sharp paring knife to trim any exposed slivers of bone from the meat. Run your hands gently around the sides to make sure no shards of bone are sticking out, and if you feel a few then use your knife to trim them out. Next, cut off any weblike layers of white fat by sliding the knife blade underneath the fat and cutting it off the shoulder. Then pat the meat dry all over with paper towels, use a towel or kitchen brush to apply white vinegar on all sides of the meat, and season all over with a healthy amount of salt and pepper.

BRISKET

Butcher shops and grocery-store meat counters break briskets down into two pieces: The first, called the "flat," comes from an area near the cow's belly and is relatively lean; the second, called the "point" cut, comes from near the shank and has more fat (and more flavor). When you are smoking a brisket, you need the whole thing, untrimmed and uncut, and that runs 12 to 15 pounds (5.4 to 6.8 kg) total and might need to be ordered in advance. If you want to make a small bris-

ket, you'll most likely find a 5-pound (2.3-kg) cut and you can follow my method exactly, but you'll need to adjust the cooking time. To make a great piece of brisket, start with a great piece of meat: I like grass-fed wagyu cattle the very best.

The first step is to trim the meat's membrane, that fine, silvery, weblike fat that covers its surface. This involves slowly cutting away the layers of sticky silver-white matter from the actual beef, and I warn you that it can be a painstaking process that requires patience and determination. But it's worth doing right, because it could make the difference between meat that's tough and meat that's tender. Also, seasonings like salt and pepper (and any rub you choose to use) won't stick to fat; the spices only adhere to the meat itself—and those spices are what create the "bark," or seared coating, that surrounds the brisket when you cook it. So take your time and carefully trim off all of the fatty membrane around that brisket before you rub it down with white vinegar and season it all over with salt and pepper.

CHICKEN

The best chickens to buy are local birds that have never been frozen and that foraged for food and ate plants (not industrially raised corn-fed birds from the freezer case, in other words). I look for big birds because they are easier to handle; 3 or even 4 pounds (1.4 to 1.8 kg) is my ideal.

I can't preach enough about how much faster and easier it is to cook a chicken if you butterfly it before you put it in your pit or smoker. You can butterfly,

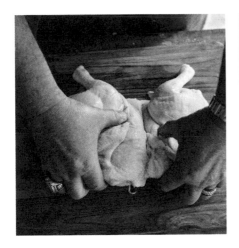

or spatchcock, as we old-school barbecue cooks like to call it, a chicken in less than a minute with just a pair of kitchen shears. You're just cutting out the backbone so that you can open up the bird, kind of like how you would crack a book. Place the chicken on a clean cutting board and turn it over so it's breast side down; the backbone runs down the center of the chicken from the neck to the tail. Starting on one side of the tail—either side is fine—cut all the way up along the spine of the chicken, exerting a little pressure to cut all the way through the bones (it shouldn't need a lot of strength to do this, it's easy). Then repeat the process by cutting up the other side. Now you've cut out the backbone, which you can either save for stock (smoke it first and your stock will be delicious) or toss out if you're feeling lazy. Flip the chicken over on your cutting board and press down on its back with the flats of your palms to flatten it out. This action should break the breastbone so that the chicken lies flat. Then you can tuck the wings under the breast so they don't dry out, and you're good to go.

With my bulldog, Winston.

ACKNOWLEDGMENTS

My list of thanks needs to be short and sweet because Dad taught me this style of cooking with no help from other family members. If you want to see the names of my other family members, they're in my first two cookbooks. Of course there are always individuals who help you through life and circumstances, but this book is about the influence of my relationship with my dad, Jack Mixon, and the path, unbeknownst to him at the time, that he set me on. Without first learning how to manage his pits, I wouldn't be the winningest man in BBQ. Thanks, Daddy.

I would like to thank my publishing house, Abrams, for believing in a cookbook that requires readers to build a pit and manage a fire, which are apparently dicey things in the world of Manhattan publishing. Publisher Michael Sand and our editor Camaren Subhiyah were terrific to work with and made sure their team respected my wishes for presenting this old-school barbecue technique. Rob Deborde is responsible for bringing the vision to life with his remarkable illustrations. Johnny Autry came down to my barbecue compound in Unadilla, Georgia, and produced the stunning photographs while I called him a hipster the whole time. Super-agent Michael Psaltis has been part of my personal pit crew for years and continues to work hard on my behalf. And Kelly Alexander is still the best food writer in the world. To all of these folks, I am deeply grateful.

ABOUT THE AUTHORS

MYRON MIXON was born into a barbecue family. His father, Jack, owned and operated a barbecue take-out business in Vienna, Georgia, which Myron helped him run. His parents sold Jack's Old South, their house brand of barbecue sauce, in their store. When Jack died unexpectedly in 1996, Myron decided to enter some barbecue contests in hopes of selling sauce. He competed in his first competition in Augusta, Georgia, later that year and took first place in Whole Hog, first place in Pork Ribs, and third in Pork Shoulder. He was hooked. Since then he has won more than 200 grand championships resulting in more than 1,900 trophies; won more than 40 state championships, including wins in Georgia, Florida, Alabama, Virginia, Arkansas, Mississippi, Kentucky, Illinois, South Carolina, and Tennessee; and has been head of Team of the Year a record eight times. In addition, he has won eleven national championships, taken three first-place whole hogs at the Jack Daniel's World Championship Invitational Barbecue Competition, and been the Grand Champion at the World Championship Memphis in May three times, in 2001, 2004, and 2007. His team is the only team to win Grand Championships in Memphis in May, the Kansas City BBQ Society, and the Florida BBQ Association in the same year.

Myron's success with his competition team, Jack's Old South, has led him to countless media appearances. He is the executive producer and host of *BBQ Rules* and star of two other hit television shows, *BBQ Pitmasters* and *BBQ Pit Wars* on Discovery's Destination America, broadcast throughout the world. Myron is the author of the hugely successful *New York Times* bestselling cookbook *Smokin' with Myron Mixon: Recipes Made Simple, from the Winningest Man in Barbecue* (Ballantine, 2011) and *Everyday Barbecue* (Ballantine, 2013). In addition, Myron has a popular line of rubs and sauces, two different lines of smokers/grills—the professional-grade line of custom Myron Mixon Smokers and the consumer-level line of Myron Mixon Pitmaster Q3 smokers—and the Myron Mixon Pitmaster Grill Tool—a combination chef knife, food flipper, and bottle opener. For more information about Myron or his products, go to: www.jacksoldsouth.com.

When he's not competing, Myron teaches barbecue at his Jack's Old South Cooking School, an intensive weekend-long course that is held several times each year. He is also a regular participant and speaker at food festivals, competitions, and events throughout the world.

Writer **KELLY ALEXANDER** grew up in a boisterous, southern-Jewish food-focused family in Atlanta, Georgia. She is coauthor of the *New York Times* bestselling cookbook *Smokin' with Myron Mixon* (Ballantine, 2011) and author of the critically acclaimed *Hometown Appetites: The Story of Clementine Paddleford, the Forgotten Food Writer Who Chronicled How America Ate* (Gotham, 2008). She is also the collaborator with *Top Chef* winner Richard Blais on the cookbook *Try This At Home* (Clarkson Potter, 2013); editor of *The Great American Cookbook*, a reissue of Clementine Paddleford's *How America Eats* (Rizzoli, 2012); author of *Peaches: A Savor the South Cookbook* (UNC Press, 2013); and coauthor of *Everyday Barbecue* with Myron Mixon (Ballantine, 2013). Her magazine work, which covers topics including obsessive collectors of Fiestaware and the cross-cultural significance of brisket, earned her a James Beard Foundation Journalism Award for magazine writing. She was a senior editor at *Saveur* magazine and an editor at *Food & Wine* and *Boston* magazines. Her writing also has appeared in the *New York Times*; *O: The Oprah Magazine*; *Gourmet*; *The New Republic*, *New York*; *Southern Living*; *Slate*; *Real Simple*; *Travel + Leisure*; and *Newsweek*, among many periodicals. Alexander teaches food writing at the Center for Documentary Studies at Duke University and can be heard chronicling food customs on *The State of Things*, which airs on North Carolina Public Radio. A graduate of Northwestern University's Medill School of Journalism, she lives in Chapel Hill, North Carolina, with her husband and two sons. She's currently a doctoral candidate in Cultural Anthropology at Duke University.

INDEX

NOTE: page numbers in *italics* refer to photographs

Published in 2016 by Stewart, Tabori & Chang
An imprint of ABRAMS

Library of Congress Control Number: 2015949283

ISBN: 978-1-61769-184-3

Editor: Camaren Subhiyah
Designer: Paul Kepple and Max Vandenberg @ Headcase Design www.headcasedesign.com
Production Manager: True Sims

The text of this book was composed in Avenir and Chronicle.

Printed and bound in the United States

10 9 8 7 6 5 4 3 2 1

Stewart, Tabori & Chang books are available at special discounts when purchased in quantity for premiums
and promotions as well as fundraising or educational use. Special editions can also be created to specification.
For details, contact specialsales@abramsbooks.com or the address below.

THE ART OF BOOKS SINCE 1949

115 West 18th Street · New York, NY 10011
www.abramsbooks.com